SPIRITUAL MASTERS FOR ALL SEASONS

D0062679

SPIRITUAL MASTERS FOR ALL SEASONS

MICHAEL FORD

HiddenSpring

Photograph of Thomas Merton by Sibylle Akers. Used with Permission of the Merton Legacy Trust and the Thomas Merton Center at Bellarmine University.

Photograph of Henri Nouwen by Frank Hamilton. Used with permission.

Cover design by Joy Taylor

Library of Congress Cataloging-in-Publication Data

Ford, Michael, date.
    Spiritual masters for all seasons / Michael Ford.
        p.   cm.
    Includes bibliographical references.
    ISBN 978-1-58768-055-7 (alk. paper)
    1. Theology. 2. Theologians. I. Title.
BT28.F66 2009
282.092′2 – dc22

2009026599

Published by
HiddenSpring
An imprint of Paulist Press
997 Macarthur Boulevard
Mahwah, New Jersey 07430

www.hiddenspringbooks.com

Printed and bound in the
United States of America

For
Kenneth and Phyllis Burge
and
Peter and Jane Huxham

The spiritual life unfolds in our "heart," our inmost self,
where our desires and decisions take shape.
It is here that we should be able to recognize
the authenticity of our Christian identity.

— *Enzo Bianchi*

Contents

Acknowledgments

Many authors would, I suspect, compare the process of writing a book to the pain and joy of giving birth (even if they do not have personal experience). No wonder Thomas Merton saw writing as a spiritual calling. But although you can feel isolated for months on end, it is always reassuring to know that your work has the blessing of others.

This book is largely inspired by a visit I made on behalf of the BBC to the Abbey of Our Lady of Gethsemani in September 2008. My deep gratitude to the monks (especially Father James Conner and Brother Patrick Hart) for their hospitality, prayers, and guidance, and to Dr. Paul Pearson, director and archivist of the Thomas Merton Center at Bellarmine University, Louisville, for his invaluable help.

I am indebted to the Archbishop of Canterbury, Dr. Rowan Williams, for finding time in his schedule to be interviewed about Merton for this study and to his press secretary, Marie Papworth, for making the arrangements.

I should like to thank warmly all those who agreed to be interviewed and whose names appear on the following pages. This project would certainly not have come to fruition without them. Special thanks for support and encouragement in various ways to Donald Allchin, Patricia Carlson, Lelia Doolan, Samantha Eades, Kristine Fleck, Margaret Ford, Nigel Ford, Jim Forest, Steve Georgiou, Keith Griffin, Ainsley Griffiths, Rosemary Grundy, Caroline Hewitt, Brenda Kimber, Beryl Lovell, Joan C. McDonald, Pam Millwood, Lyn Morgan, Anand Nayak, Nóirín Ní Riain, Mark O'Brien, Prashant Olalekar, Tim Pike, Silvia Reeves, Anthony Redmond, Grainne Ross, Michael Smith, Bruce Thompson, David Torevell, Gerald Twomey, Carlos Vallés, Margaret Wakeley, Tom Ward, Richard Wilkinson, and Martin Wroe.

Father Peter-Michael Scott invited me to speak about the spirituality of Henri Nouwen to the members of St. Peter's Catholic Church, Big Pine Key, Florida, where he was helping out during the summer of 2008. Then, in March 2009, I gave a Lenten presentation on Nouwen to members of Father Peter's own parish, St. John Fisher, Shepperton, South West London. That same week, I talked about Merton and Nouwen at St. Benet's Catholic Church, Abbey Wood, South East London, at the invitation of the parish priest, Father David Camilleri. On all four occasions, the words of the spiritual masters seemed to touch people in profound ways, and I am grateful for those opportunities to share their message.

Richard Keeble, professor of journalism at the University of Lincoln, UK, has supported my postdoctoral work in spirituality and journalism. I am pleased to be a Visiting Fellow, sharing my research with students and speaking to the Institute of Communication Ethics, of which Richard is a director.

This book — the fruit of journalistic experience and theological reflection — is dedicated to four people who symbolize these fields of interest. When I was a young feature writer for the *Somerset County Gazette* series in the West of England, I worked closely with the editor in chief, Ken Burge, and his wife, Phyllis, a subeditor. They became more than colleagues and have always taken a close, personal interest in my journey. Canon Peter Huxham and his wife, Jane, have also been trusted friends. I got to know Father Peter when he was lead chaplain at Musgrove Park Hospital, Taunton, where he was a devoted pastor to the sick, dying, and bereaved. We shared many memorable celebrations of the Eucharist in the chapel, especially our annual "Christmas Triduum."

Finally, my warm thanks to Paul McMahon, managing editor at Paulist Press, who helped bring this book to birth with his usual equanimity and grace, and to John Eagleson and the Paulist production team for their kindness and professionalism.

Prelude

They were intense and passionate artists, each with a distinctive brand of spiritual music. But, like the best names in jazz, they form a formidable quartet, and in this book appear together. As international spiritual guides and best-selling authors, Thomas Merton, Henri Nouwen, Anthony de Mello, and John O'Donohue caught the imagination of audiences around the world, crossing cultural and religious boundaries to extraordinary effect. Connoisseurs on the treasures of the inner life, they continue to appeal, not only to people rooted in a particular tradition, but also to those who linger on the thresholds, whether of faith and doubt, belonging and alienation, or life and death. In times of recession, their writings challenge the perception that life is little more than a consumptive enterprise.

Merton (1915–1968), de Mello (1931–1987), Nouwen (1932–1996) and O'Donohue (1956–2008) were arguably the most influential spiritual figures of recent times. Although each had a markedly different personality with a distinctive outlook, there was much in common between them. As young men, they were all ordained as Roman Catholic priests, but it was through their books that they achieved fame. Then, after making their mark on the world, all four died unexpectedly at the height of their powers while on the threshold of new discoveries — about themselves and about religion itself. Each died while traveling, far away from the places they called home.

All four were highly creative luminaries who revealed God in new and sometimes unexpected ways. In the process, they had to face their own complexities and sometimes courted controversy. Merton was a Trappist monk and civil rights campaigner who denounced U.S. policy in Vietnam and the nuclear arms race. In his final years he became a hermit, deepening his interest in Buddhism. Some have seen a correlation between his prophetic spirituality and the political philosophy of the U.S. president Barack Obama.

Nouwen, who was educated by the Jesuits and undertook the thirty-day Ignatian retreats, was a clinical psychologist and Ivy League professor of pastoral theology who gave up academia to become a pastor among people with developmental disabilities. He was the proverbial "wounded healer" who wrote more than forty books, filtering the spiritual life through a psychological prism. His ecumenical spirit, especially with regard to the sacraments, shocked some but delighted others. In his later years he followed a South African trapeze troupe across Europe and developed his most original theology from inside a circus tent. A preacher who appealed as much to the Religious Right as the Religious Left, he was invited to speak at a U.S. Congress prayer breakfast and could count both Nancy Reagan and Hillary Clinton among his loyal readers.

De Mello was a consummate storyteller and spiritual director from India, whose captivating and sometimes shocking tales were turned into paperbacks and sold in their millions. Some felt he moved away from Christianity and drew too readily from the Asian spiritual traditions. Years after his death, the Vatican investigated his writings. But some argued that the Jesuit was misunderstood in Rome and remained a loyal priest of the church.

O'Donohue was an Irish philosopher-poet who made his name through his first best seller, *Anam Ċara*. Although he eventually resigned from the priesthood, he retained a deep love of Catholicism but, like the other three, had concerns about its hierarchical trappings. He too became a hugely popular writer and speaker, especially in America, where his words live on. En route to Washington, DC, for his presidential inauguration, Barack Obama stopped in Baltimore to be greeted by governor Martin O'Malley, who offered him "A Blessing for One Who Holds Power," written by O'Donohue. It spoke of the gift of leadership awakening an inner sense of vocation. The prayer asked that the new president's work might be "infused with passion and creativity," and that it might have "the wisdom to balance compassion and challenge":

May your power never become a shell
Wherein your heart would silently atrophy.

May you welcome your own vulnerability
As the ground where healing and truth join.

May integrity of soul be your first ideal,
The source that will guide and bless your work.[1]

While O'Donohue, de Mello, Nouwen, and Merton were born far from the United States, they spoke expressively to Americans searching for the spiritual in an increasingly secular environment. Their lexicon of the inner life helped people experience a sense of personal transformation in their quest for God. At a time of economic uncertainty, when many are anxious, not only about the future, but also about the present, their words both inspire and reassure. Downturns can lead to depressions of many kinds, but they can also be *kairos* moments, occasions for growth and renewal. Although these authors offer a spiritual compass to guide people through the winter of their lives, they are men for all seasons who understand the language of interiority and provide nourishment at any time.

The idea for this book was conceived as the forty-fourth president of the United States — "amidst gathering clouds and raging storms" — urged the American nation to "begin again the work of remaking America." As Obama explained that this would involve remaining faithful to ancestral ideals, joining imagination to common purpose, and necessity to courage, I began to sense that the four writers, whose books filled my shelves, could offer, in counterpoint, a spiritual accompaniment to the emerging political melody.

President Obama spelled out the reality. America was at war against a global network of violence and hatred, while the economy — along with health care, education, and the environment — was in deep crisis. No less profound was a sapping of confidence and a fear that the nation's decline was inevitable.

On that bitingly cold January morning of 2009, there was also a perceptible vein of spirituality flowing through the body of his speech. The crowds had gathered because they had chosen hope over fear, unity of purpose over conflict and discord.

"We remain a young nation," said the politician-preacher, "but in the words of Scripture, the time has come to set aside childish things. The time has come to reaffirm our enduring spirit; to choose our better history; to carry forward that precious gift, that noble idea, passed on from generation to generation: the God-given promise that all are equal, all are free, and all deserve a chance to pursue their full measure of happiness."

In reaffirming the greatness of America, its inhabitants understood that greatness was never a given. It had to be earned. Time and again the nation's forebears had struggled and sacrificed — "worked till their hands were raw" — so that Americans could live a better life. They had been able to see the nation as bigger than the sum of individual ambitions, greater than all the differences of birth, wealth, or faction. It was the common good that mattered.

President Obama pointed out that, in its poise for renewed leadership in the world, America would be a friend of every nation and every person who sought a future of peace and dignity. Its ancestors had known that power grew through prudence and that security arose from the justness of the cause, the force of example and "the tempering qualities" of humility and restraint. "We are the keepers of this legacy," he declared.

America's patchwork heritage was a strength, not a weakness. It was a nation of Christians and Muslims, Jews, Hindus, and nonbelievers, shaped by every language and culture. Just as it had tasted the "bitter swill of civil war and segregation, and emerged from that dark chapter stronger and more united," so the United States had to believe that old hatreds and tribal divisions would eventually dissolve. Furthermore, America had a crucial role in ushering in a new era of peace. The reconciliatory and compassionate fabric of the Christian gospel seemed woven into his words as President Obama addressed followers of Islam: "To the Muslim world, we seek a new way forward, based on mutual interest and mutual respect. To those leaders around the globe who seek to sow conflict, or blame their society's ills on the West — know that your people will judge you on what you can build, not what you destroy. To those who cling to power through corruption and deceit and the silencing of dissent, know that you are on the wrong side of history; but that we will extend a hand if you are willing to unclench your fist. To the people of poor nations, we pledge to work alongside you to make your farms flourish and let clean waters flow; to nourish starved bodies and feed hungry minds. And to those nations like ours that enjoy relative plenty, we say we can no longer afford indifference to the suffering outside our borders; nor can we consume the world's resources without regard to effect. For the world has changed, and we must change with it."

The president went on: "As we consider the road that unfolds before us, we remember with humble gratitude those brave Americans who, at this very hour, patrol far-off deserts and distant mountains. They have something to tell us, just as the fallen heroes who lie in Arlington whisper through the ages. We honor them not only because they are guardians of our liberty, but because they embody the spirit of service; a willingness to find meaning in something greater than themselves. And yet, at this moment — a moment that will define a generation — it is precisely this spirit that must inhabit us all."

Obama said it was ultimately "the faith and determination" of the American people on which the nation relied in dark times, such as individual acts of kindness to a stranger or the collective selflessness of a workforce keener to cut back on their own hours than see a colleague lose a job. The source of America's confidence lay in the knowledge that "God calls on us to shape an uncertain destiny." Hope and virtue would be anchors in the approaching storms, the new president counseled, and Americans should be unfaltering as they carried "that great gift of freedom" to future generations "with eyes fixed on the horizon and God's grace upon us." He seemed intent on reuniting a divided nation and healing a broken world. It was not music to the ears of the cynics, but it was definitely in the spirit of the kings and queens of jazz. The trumpeter and composer Wynton Marsalis, a fellow African American of the same generation, said Obama's message had always been about bringing people together and that was a major strand in the philosophy of the American jazz tradition.

As I toasted Obama's health at home in England, I found myself transfixed to a large flat screen as high-definition images of the historic day were beamed around the world. It was not merely the visible and audible challenge of the speech that engulfed my attention, but the latent call for inner transformation. Somehow Obama reminded me so much of Merton, who had been America's best-known contemplative in the mid-twentieth century and had written so prolifically and prophetically about civil rights, nonviolence, interfaith dialogue, and, above all, about the need to find one's true self in God. Meanwhile, at his home beside the mountains of North Wales, in the United Kingdom, another writer was feeling much the same way. "The world needs Barack Obama — and the world needs Thomas Merton," said Canon A. M. (Donald) Allchin who had been with Merton at the time of Martin Luther King's assassination. He was not the only person to make an immediate connection.

On February 5, 2009, an Internet blogger, Mark Shaw, said he felt Obama's words at the National Prayer Breakfast would have been appreciated by Thomas Merton: "I was not raised in a particularly religious household. I had a father who was born a Muslim but became an atheist, grandparents who were non-practicing Methodists and Baptists, and a mother who was skeptical of organized religion, even as she was the kindest, most spiritual person I've ever known. She was the one who taught me as a child to love, and to understand, and to do unto others as I would want done. I didn't become a Christian until many years later, when I moved to the South Side of Chicago after college. It happened not because of indoctrination or a sudden revelation, but because I spent month after month working with church folks who simply wanted to help neighbors who were down on their luck — no matter what they looked like, or where they came from, or who they prayed to. It was on those streets, in those neighborhoods, that I first heard God's spirit beckon me. It was there that I felt called to a higher purpose — His purpose."

Father James Conner, who worked closely with Merton at the Abbey of Our Lady of Gethsemani in Kentucky, said Merton had touched on the oneness of humanity and the dignity of each person. That was why he had been so zealous for racial justice and peace and so against war and nuclear arms. To that extent, Father Conner believed Merton could be a spiritual guide for the remaking of America under Obama. "I think that he would delight in the way that Obama has shown an openness to other nations and cultures, as was seen in the Inter-Americas Conference and his dealings with President Hugo Chávez of Venezuela, as well as his attempts to open doors with Cuba and Iran. Merton would have hoped that, through Obama, America could come to respect all peoples and all cultures, and to see the dignity of each person in the sense that they are truly a part of ourselves."

In July 2009, Obama told America's oldest civil rights organization that African Americans should take charge of their own lives. In his first presidential speech on race, Obama said: "Government programs alone won't get our children to the promised land — we need a new mindset, a new set of attitudes." His words were described by one journalist as "passionate, even preacher-like."

As a theology student in Britain in the 1980s, I was fortunate to study Merton in my final year. Throughout my university days a framed picture of the habited contemplative on stood the left-hand corner of my desk. I used to look up at him for inspiration as I typed my essays about his life and times. No one in the faculty was an authority on Merton, so this meant long hours of solitary study in the university library or alone in my flat, followed by weekends rummaging through second-hand bookshops for what copies of books I could find. As none of the excellent teaching staff was a specialist in the area, I was asked if I would like to supply my own examination questions, an invitation that did not extend to the marking. Following graduation, however, I began to drift away from the texts that had sated me intellectually. After an intense academic relationship with Merton, I knew I had to move on.

Then, in the summer of 2008, I found myself rediscovering Merton in preparation for a BBC Radio 4 program on the fortieth anniversary of the monk's death. I summoned the courage to glance through my old essays, and my affinity with Merton was swiftly rekindled although this time, I sensed, in a more spiritual way. With producer Mark O'Brien, I traveled to the Abbey of Gethsemani, where we recorded sequences with the monks who had known Merton and later spent time in New York capturing the jazz-infused mood of his adolescence. Some of these stories appear in the book.

My first recorded Radio 4 program featured the spiritual writer Henri Nouwen, who had been much influenced by Merton. I have drawn from our conversation for his portrait. Later, in the course of my biographical research on Nouwen, I interviewed 125 people, but it was not possible to include everything in *Wounded Prophet*,[2] so new material is presented here for the first time.

A few years ago I started looking into the possibility of writing a book on Anthony de Mello who, intriguingly, had never been the subject of a critical biography. I had many of his books but knew little about his character and background. With a view to a biography, I interviewed a number of people from India, Spain, and the United States, but the project was hampered by difficulties and eventually shelved. In my assessment of de Mello, I have drawn on these unpublished reflections.

Always at home with the Celtic imagination, I appreciated John O'Donohue's gentle and perceptive writing about the outer and inner landscapes of people's lives. After the success of his first book, *Anam Ċara*, I interviewed him at his home on the west coast of Ireland. As always, I returned to the studios with more material than I could possibly use, but those tapes have formed the basis of his profile here.

A synthesis of personal reminiscence and theological reflection, this book offers fresh insights into the souls of these popular authors whose spiritual writings act as torches for an exploration of the interior world. The style is both conversational and analytical as each portrait examines the character and the message of its subject. It is, of course, impossible to incorporate, within these short cameos, every facet or angle, but I hope that, in lifting the curtain on these four writers as a quartet, the stage is set for further study and investigation. There is no substitute for the primary sources and each of the four deserves a careful reading.

As you will discover, even for the most stimulating of guides, the spiritual journey is often trod with feet of clay. This alone should give us heart. All four writers wrestled with their demons from time to time and each found some aspects of institutional religion a stumbling block on the road to authentic spiritual living. But, grounded as they were in their own Catholic faith, especially its mystical guise, they discovered within themselves an inner freedom to push boundaries and explore lands beyond. Struggles were recurring contours in their spiritual topography but, refusing to see them as obstacles, they owned them as noble routes to the transcendent.

These four visionaries spoke and wrote voluminously. Admittedly, not everyone identified with their spirituality or their style of expressing it, but many others did and were transformed in the process. What all four shared in life as compelling communicators of the Christian faith, they continue to share in death, as their books keep selling across the world, despite a global recession. In this study, a blend of the spiritual and the journalistic, their outer characters and inner convictions are explored within a single volume. There are engaging connections and differences. For example, while Nouwen and de Mello draw on psychology, Merton and de Mello mine Asian spiritual traditions. O'Donohue and Merton are linked because they were poets, Nouwen and O'Donohue coincide in their thoughts on benediction. Film directors in America are said to have sought counsel from O'Donohue; one young Hollywood actor was named in baptism after Merton. De Mello was a man from the East who died in the West. Merton was a man from the West who died in the East. And so on.

In the world of jazz, four unique voices can come together to form a distinctive sound, with each of their instruments fulfilling a different role. As well as their ability to express their own voice, the players listen closely to other members of the quartet and are able to meld. Here, Thomas Merton, Henri Nouwen, Anthony de Mello, and John O'Donohue share a platform, offering a vibrant spiritual score, not only for the age of Obama, but for all times.

ONE

Unmasking the Self

The Faces of Thomas Merton

Paradoxically, I have found peace because I have always been dissatisfied. My moments of depression and despair turn out to be renewals, new beginnings.[1]

Thomas Merton was a monk who adored his jazz. He liked its power, unity, and drive. But he also knew that music helped him speak of other realities. Like the "High Priest of Bebop," Thelonious Monk, who had his own inimitable style, Thomas Merton was a unique solo performer with a highly original repertoire. They had more in common than their initials. But behind his own four walls, Merton was more at home with the music of Ornette Coleman and Jackie McLean, whose records were as much companions as the works of St. Thomas Aquinas and St. John of the Cross. The quiet hermitage in the woods, where he went to explore silence and solitude, could sometimes sound like Birdland.

In fact, I felt I could almost hear the faint sound of a saxophone as I approached the pyramid-shaped hills of Kentucky in a corner of the United States noted more for its production of Bourbon whiskey than the contemplative musings of a jazz-loving genius. I remember my excitement that hot September afternoon, traveling beside neatly harvested cornfields and towering oaks, as I suddenly caught sight of the white-faced Abbey of Our Lady of Gethsemani shyly emerging through the trees.

After many years imagining what Merton's enclosed world must have looked like, it was hard to believe I was finally arriving at the monastery where the twenty-six-year-old novice had begun a journey that would radically change not only his own life but the lives of many others too. I had passed the jazz clubs of Greenwich Village that Merton had frequented in his more self-indulgent days. Now I was eight hundred miles away from New York, sizing up an enclosure that had somehow managed to contain not only the most influential American Catholic author of the twentieth century but also a fearless global campaigner for peace and social justice. On the flight from La Guardia to the city of Louisville, where Merton had applauded jazz musicians, I reminded myself of his story. It seemed to have all the spiritual passion of *A Love Supreme* by John Coltrane. Like Merton himself, Coltrane was a constant searcher who believed in common essences.

Born at Prades in the French Pyrenees on January 31, 1915, Thomas Merton was the son of traveling artists. His New Zealand-born father, Owen Merton, and his American-born mother, Ruth Jenkins, had met at a painting school in Paris and been married at St. Anne's Church in the Soho district of London — the heart of Britain's jazz land. Educated in England at Oakham Public School (where Tom played jazz loudly on his record player) and, briefly, at Clare College, Cambridge, the young Merton found his life spiraling out of control as he indulged in a hedonistic lifestyle of drinking and debauchery. He was even rumored to have fathered an illegitimate child. Supported by an independent income after the death of his parents, he behaved like a spoiled kid in a time of recession.

But in his twenties, while a student at Columbia University, Merton eventually became more disciplined as he began to feel shame for his former life. Intellectual thinkers and friends influenced his conversion to Roman Catholicism. He said that, in spiritual terms, the decision came about through the divine actions of grace and mercy. First there was a realization of God's infinite Being and presence, then of Christ as God's son and redeemer, living in the church.

Two years after the outbreak of the Second World War, Merton entered Gethsemani, a community within the Order of Cistercians of the Strict Observance (known as Trappists), where he prayed that his "rebellious sins and ingratitude" might be "burned away."

In this sanctified enclosure, far from the tainted world, he confronted the miseries, mistakes, and confusions of his past life and began a long journey of inner transformation. His ensuing twenty-seven years as a monk brought about profound changes in Merton's self-understanding and, in the process, he emerged as an eloquent spiritual writer and social critic of international stature. Ironically, the more he moved into silence, the more he felt compelled to write. The pen became his voice. Merton's autobiography, *The Seven Storey Mountain,* which his abbot directed him to write, was published in 1948, selling six hundred thousand copies in the first year alone. With a hundred or more books to follow, Merton's writings were to bring him fame that he had neither predicted nor desired. They also provided an important source of income for the monastery as well as a number of new postulants.

At the time, vast numbers of servicemen had been returning from wars in Europe and the Far East, while others were struggling to come to terms with the devastating effect of nuclear weapons on Hiroshima and Nagasaki. The horrors of Nazi concentration camps and the Holocaust were coming to light. There was a changing world geography with the formation of the State of Israel, the partition of India, the rise of communism, and the raising of the Iron and Bamboo Curtains. It was against this background that Merton turned his back on the world and found meaning within a rural monastery. Through his books he introduced vast numbers to the contemplative tradition within Christianity, especially to the writings of the church fathers and the great Christian mystics.

Described as the conscience of the peace movement in the 1960s and a "theologian of resistance,"[2] Merton was a strong supporter of nonviolent civil rights, which he considered the greatest example of Christian faith in action in the social history of the United States. He also put his head above the monastic parapet in his protests against U.S. policy in Vietnam and the nuclear arms race. But despite a popular following, Merton found himself severely criticized by both Catholics and non-Catholics, who condemned his social activism as unbecoming of a monk. Some of his writings were censored by the monastic authorities.

Merton also immersed himself in the study of Asian religions, particularly Zen Buddhism, and the promotion of East-West dialogue. After several meetings with Merton, the Dalai Lama praised him as having a more profound understanding of Buddhism than any other Christian he had known.

Toward the end of his life, Merton fell in love with a young nurse but later reaffirmed his monastic vows. It was the stuff of movies, but the monk resisted interest from Hollywood in turning his life into a motion picture and was always curious why his books sold so well in that corner of California. More than forty years after his death, he is still read avidly across the world, while every year up to three thousand people visit Bellarmine University in Louisville to do research in the Merton archives. While Merton would have been gladdened by any serious study, application, or development of his ideas, he was never remotely interested in becoming an icon. He said he aimed not at the heights but at the depths, aspiring to be a nonentity and someone who would be forgotten. There were many ironies and paradoxes in the world of Thomas Merton.

Encountering the Mystery

On a walk through the exterior and interior worlds of the abbey, Brother Paul Quenon, who was a novice under Merton, explained how his teacher had originally entered the monastery to seek catharsis. "You come here to find purity of heart so there is continual cleansing," he told me. "You might go through moments when you think you've got it, then that slowly fades. It is a process more than a state. Of course going into the monastery is almost like what some people experience when they are embraced by their mothers. It might be somewhat terrifying, like walking into a prison — you don't know what you're going into. But when Merton came to the monastery, he began very quickly to feel that this was a paradise. He wrote with great enthusiasm about how Gethsemani was the center of America. Everything revolved around it. I think he later regretted that hyperbole." Nonetheless, even in the 1960s, Merton would write that he still had a strange sense that Providence had brought him to the monastery. He felt he belonged to the land around Gethsemani with its rocky hills and pine trees. Within those woods and fields, he had encountered the deepest mystery of his own life. It was a place chosen not by him, but for him.

"Merton was constantly rediscovering God," said Brother Paul. "He was always pushing back the horizons, exploring the boundaries and bringing the rest of us along with him. He got to know himself as unknown and perhaps even unknowable. One of his deep insights was that the mystery of God is continuous with the mystery of the self. So we can never really know ourselves except in terms of God and, of course, who can know God? So it was a continual expansion into the unknown. The unknowability of the self is really a reflection, a mirror of the unknowability of God."

Thomas Merton was, then, one of the greatest exponents of the apophatic tradition in Christian spirituality, a guide to those who experience crises of faith and doubt in their lives. Echoing the mystical theology of St. John of the Cross, Merton speaks of "the curtain of darkness," "the night of aridity and faith," and the "power of an obscure love." The Dark Night is a turning point on the spiritual journey as we are beckoned to move away from our safety and defenses, beyond our limits and beyond our selves. The way of faith involves traveling by night. The closer we get to God, the less our faith is diluted with the half-light of created images and concepts. The more obscure the path becomes, the greater the certainty. While the journey may cause anguish and doubt, it is in the deepest darkness that we possess God most fully. We are filled with God's infinite light, which, to our own reasoning, seems like pure darkness.

According to Thomas Merton, a monk's life should remain hidden in God, mysterious and stripped, but always expressing truth and simplicity before, with, and in the divine. He saw himself as one of a rare breed of contemplative priests who sought pure union with God. As a writer on interiority, he "spoke out for the inside." He assumed correctly that most of his readers were people who instinctively felt there was more to life than they were experiencing. He wanted to tell them about a deeper reality that they could discover within themselves if only they looked carefully enough. But Merton was astute enough to point out that the very circumstances of their lives might prevent people from being able to detect and unveil this interior dimension. Merton realized that women and men could exist almost entirely at the superficial level without an awareness of the inner depths of their being. But there could be no real love of life unless it were oriented toward the discovery of one's true, spiritual self, a process often hampered, if not blocked, by a perfunctory concentration on external joys and fears. But when the road toward interiority was opened up and people began to live in communion with the unknown in them, they would taste freedom.

At the core of Merton's spirituality lies the distinction between our real and false selves. The false self is the identity we assume in order to function in society, the springboard of all our egocentric desires such as honor, power, and knowledge. We expend our energies constructing this nothingness into something objectively real. If we take our masks to be our true faces, observes Merton, we will protect them with the bandages of pleasures and glory, even at the cost of violating our own truth. If we do not know who we are, it is because we live out the fantasies of what everyone else wants us to be. But the real self, toward which we should move, is a religious mystery, known only in its entirety by God. The deep secrecy of our own being is often hidden from us by our own estimates or illusions of what we are. The way to find the real "world" is not about observing what is outside us but about discovering our own inner ground. For that, says Merton, is where the world is first and foremost — in our deepest selves. It not a visible, determined structure with fixed laws but a living and self-creating mystery of which we are all a part and to which we have our own unique doors. Merton writes:

> The only true joy on earth is to escape from the prison of our own false self and enter by love into union with the Life Who

dwells and sings within the essence of every creature and in the core of our own souls. In His love we possess all things and enjoy fruition of them, finding Him in them all. And thus as we go about the world, everything we meet and everything we see and hear and touch, far from defiling, purifies us and plants in us something more of contemplation and of heaven.

Short of this perfection, created things do not bring us joy but pain. Until we love God perfectly, everything in the world will be able to hurt us. And the greatest misfortune is to be dead to the pain they inflict on us, and not realize what it is.[3]

The Wisdom of Suffering

Sitting behind the reception desk in the guest house at Gethsemani, Father Matthew Kelty, who was born in the same year as Merton, told me that he thought the writer was a true spiritual guide for these times because, through him, many had concluded that "there's more than what you see, you know." Merton encouraged people to listen to their inner voice and not imitate the behavior of people around them. Merton's life had been a love affair with God. Every now and then God did that, said Father Matthew. "He was a man of God, and he realized how funny God was because he was just an ordinary man. There was nothing special about him."

Father Matthew, who joined the order in June 1960, completed his novitiate under Merton and was later his confessor. He had learned that, back in the 1940s, the rigors of monastic living retained a medieval aroma. "It smelt...of incense and wet wool," he said. "You know what a dog smells like when it's wet? That — and the incense combined. They didn't open the windows all winter and they had very little heat. In the cold, wool gets damp and the dormitory was damp. The monks slept on straw mattresses — that wasn't too bad. They changed them every few months. Merton needed discipline and, as he figured it was good for him, he accepted it. But he suffered from lack of privacy and couldn't sleep with others because of the snoring, so he had a little cubicle built over the stairway. It was just a room, a hideaway. He was not favored but, from the beginning, his health was poor. He had a sensitive stomach, so he was given special diets. He kept the regular monastic hours. He was very faithful and went to choir. He got up at quarter to three in the morning — may have been two then.

"He never wasted a minute. He would put you to shame for his zeal. He read a lot at different times of the day. We didn't think of him being repentant for his past life. He was humble, gentle, and obedient. But he could be British. The British have a capacity for cutting you down, but they do it with style. He could do that, not very often, but he could do it. He was witty in a British way — it was a bright humor.

"He was very creative. He had a new idea every month for some project or another. He would go to see the abbot who would listen as he talked and talked. And at the end, the abbot would turn down his suggestion, so Merton would dry his tears and try again. In the sixties, he would sometimes overdo it though. He would go out and picnic, drink beer and sort of show off that he was open to anything. But he became more benign, more human. He was a very honest person who didn't stand out from the other brothers. You wouldn't know who he was. He wasn't special in that sense. The proof of that lay in the fact that the monks made nothing of him because he didn't make anything of himself. He was not our famous writer and poet — or our holy mystic. He was just one of the boys."

Merton had the hearing of the superiors who respected his intellectual acumen. He was more learned than most in the monastery and could speak many languages. But he did not like to be interrupted, said Father Matthew. "We were told as novices: 'Never bother a monk when he's working. Leave him alone.' Merton was demanding. I used to have to type for him because he never had a secretary until the last year of his life. He would give me letters to type. You couldn't read his writing. He was a devil to work for. He would have his manuscript in one place, then he would add stuff and put it on the back of something else which you wouldn't see so you had to do it again because you'd miss something. His handwriting was wretched and he'd have a word like 'Albuquerque,' which I couldn't read. So I would have to go and knock on his door. But he wouldn't like it. He'd look at you like you were somebody your mother had dropped when you were a baby. He didn't suffer fools gladly. But basically he was a good person."

Father Matthew described Merton as someone who had grown up "ignorant, pagan, rich, and spoiled." He had suffered a miserable, wandering childhood and had not enjoyed a traditional family life. His mother, father, and brother had all died at young ages. "He had a lot of sadness and you'd see it in his face if you knew when to look. Some of his pictures reveal it. There's a certain sadness in him at the beginning of his monastic life. But all monks have known suffering. That is where they get their wisdom from.

"This place had two hundred monks after World War II. If you had been through the war, you couldn't go back to a frivolous life. The monks here wanted something with meaning. Today in society we don't have that. Some people don't have a deep thought. Suffering makes us more compassionate people or else it turns you bitter. That was Merton's key. He used it to become more Christlike because Christ pointed to the beauty of the suffering in his own life. Merton's life was something like a transfiguration, and he was very grateful to God. If he'd have stayed in New York, he'd have been a dreadful person. He would have been a typical Briton in the worst sense — snobbish, smart, wealthy, intelligent, and quick lipped, the worldly type. But Merton did not pretend. He tried to see the meaning of what the life here was about. He was real, and his suffering made it real for him. Many people have found God because of him."

The Echo of Silence

Thomas Merton never completely adjusted to the monastic rhythm, exhibiting a restlessness throughout his life. Being at odds was more his temper. Not that he was a difficult man, except, perhaps, on occasions in dealing with his superior, but even then he would be diplomatic. He was jovial, buoyant, and a lot of fun to be with, but he did not like the childish behavior of some monks. A free spirit, he helped loosen his fellow brothers. He helped renew monastic structures, shifting the emphasis away from penance and more toward contemplation, which he viewed as the highest expression of the intellectual and spiritual life. Contemplation was spiritual wonder and spontaneous awe at the sacredness of life and of being. For him, the life and being that existed in every person proceeded from an invisible, transcendent, and infinitely abundant Source. Contemplation was, above all, an awareness of the reality of that Source, a vision to which both reason and faith aspired. And yet, of course, contemplation could not, in fact, be classed as a vision as such because it saw "without seeing" and knew "without knowing." Contemplation was not the fruit of anyone's efforts or a form of self-hypnosis achieved by concentrating on one's own inner spiritual being but a transcendent gift — the religious apprehension of God, through life in God. It was the awareness and, to some degree, experience of what every Christian obscurely believed. Hence, writes Merton:

> Contemplation is more than a consideration of abstract truths about God, more even than affective meditation on the things we believe. It is awakening, enlightenment and the amazing intuitive grasp by which love gains certitude of God's creative and dynamic intervention in our daily life. Hence contemplation does not simply "find" a clear idea of God and confine Him within the limits of that idea, and Hold him there as a prisoner to Whom it can always return. On the contrary, contemplation is carried away by Him into His own realm, His own mystery and His own freedom. It is a pure and virginal knowledge, poor in concepts, poorer still in reasoning, but able, by its very poverty and purity, to follow the Word "wherever He may go."[4]

For Merton, contemplation is not a philosophy or a science but a response to a call or, more precisely, the echo of a silent voice resonating in the inmost center of our spirit. It is as if, in creating us,

God has asked a question and, in awakening us to contemplation, God has answered that question so that the contemplative becomes, at the same time, both question and answer.

But in the everyday life of Gethsemani, Father Louis — Merton was given the name Louis when he received the novice habit — had also to experience the more mundane face of monasticism. Despite his health problems, he worked vigorously, loading hay bales as efficiently as monks who were much younger. Merton, always fond of trees, was also the forester. (He once said that, as marginal people in a technological world, monks should see themselves as trees that exist silently in the dark and purify the air). "We had a great time as novices, trooping out in a line with axes under our arms to thin out the woods for the health of the existing trees," recalled Brother Paul. "We would get on the end of a six-foot saw and cut the logs. We also had a small tobacco plantation, a limited field of ten acres at most. That was standard in Kentucky. Everyone had to have a tobacco plot because that's how you made your money on a farm. The monks cut tobacco by hand with machetes. Merton loathed noisy equipment and complained loudly about it. But I think he loved the silence."

One of Merton's many paradoxes was that, while he desired solitude, he also valued the company of friends whose conversations stimulated him. These encounters enabled him to share insights he had gleaned through the monastic life. Merton seems to have needed the social dynamic and the aloneness in equal measure. Another paradox was that contemplation was sometimes a struggle, while struggle itself could sometimes be a form of contemplation. Merton told novices how faith was really about grappling with God in much the same way as Jacob had wrestled with an angel — "and you don't know who's going to come out on top." Merton did not see paradox as a contradiction but more as a duality of meanings.

After attending the afternoon office of None in the monastery chapel, I was introduced to Father James Conner who first met Merton shortly after he entered Gethsemani in August 1949. At the time he hadn't read *The Seven Storey Mountain* but knew about the book and "wondered who that monk was." Eventually a brother pointed him out in Chapter. Merton was sitting across from James Conner, who began to observe him during the abbot's talks. He appeared lively and showed his reactions readily in facial expressions and sometimes by signs. The monks used sign language at that time because of the strict rules of silence. Ever the artist, Merton devised his own style.

A year or so later Merton was assigned to give talks to the novices on early monastic history. Although he presented only one lecture a week, it was always of a high standard and the brothers delighted in it. Merton was extremely well prepared and had an animated, jovial style of delivery. But after a few months the talks suddenly came to an end because the novice master claimed that they were impinging on his unique relationship with the novices. "I think there was some friction because he realized how much the novices enjoyed Merton's conferences in contrast to his own," Father James recalled. "The following year, 1951, Merton was appointed to a new position as master of students. At that time all of the 'choir religious' automatically pursued studies for priesthood, so there was a group of about twenty-five monks who were in temporary vows or also solemn vows as they prepared for ordination. In October of that year, I made my first vows and came under him as father master. The students met him at least once a month privately, and he also gave an excellent conference every Sunday afternoon about our life as monks and as students for priesthood. We were also given the option to choose him for our own personal confessor, which meant we could meet him each week for confession and spiritual direction. It was during that time that my relationship with him developed most.

"He was a real 'lifesaver' for me at the time. He had an unusual ability to perceive where I was and what was happening. Up until then, it had always been the custom that, whenever you went to speak to the abbot or father master, you always knelt the whole time. So the first occasion I went in to see Merton, I knelt as he gave me the traditional blessing and then he said: 'Sit Down!' That was a real revelation to me. It showed the respect he had for the person. He felt monks should be able to speak person to person, and not just in a position of submission. Eventually that was accepted even by the abbot, but at the time it was unheard of. Merton showed that same respect to everyone. He tried to help us learn how to have respect for one another, even toward those in the community who might have seemed more difficult."

Merton was James Conner's confessor and director for four years until Merton became novice master. After being ordained a priest in 1957, Father James assisted Merton as undermaster for novices for three years. It was different working with him on that level, more as equals than as father master. "He was always very open and friendly, sharing with me some of the things which were going on in his own life at that time," said Father James.

"I appreciated that very much. I think that the priesthood meant a great deal to Merton, particularly in being able to celebrate Mass. He always had a great devotion to the Eucharist. I think he delighted in his priesthood. I remember when I was ordained; he sent me a small holy card with a note on the back. It said: 'I am sure that today is the happiest day of your life.' I think that reflected him as well as it might have me. At the same time, though, I do recall reading that he remarked something to the effect that he felt that the greatest problems he encountered came as a result of his priesthood."

Penetrating Eternity

Father James said Merton had taught him to be a monk — and how to discover who he was and who God called him to be. One of his teacher's great gifts had been the ability to be a spiritual person without sacrificing anything of his own humanity. The fact that Merton still spoke powerfully to so many was evidence that he had lived the very solitude of which he had written, a solitude that had led him, not only into his own heart, but also into the heart of every person with whom he was one in Christ. Father James remembered that, when Merton was master of students, he liked to head off to the woods for solitude. "But he would invite those of us who were students to join him there for an hour after dinner. We would go out and then separate each to our own place in the woods. At the end of the hour he would ring a bell that he had erected in the woods to warn us that it was time for the next Office. In this way Merton was able to have his solitude and yet also share it with us as a way of teaching the beauty of solitude in nature. This expressed something of the combination of his love for solitude and love of community but principally he had sought a life in a community where he could find the God who first sought him.

"Merton's whole life was centered on the divine mercy which led him into his search for solitude. But he found much more in solitude than merely a *peace* that he sought. He discovered there his own heart with all of its darkness and light commingled as the dwelling place of God. There, also, was the heart of all humanity."

Merton says that, to seek solitude, you do not have to be constantly traveling from one geographical possibility to another. You are a solitary the moment you become aware of your own actual, inalienable solitude that will never disappear. He does not think that, in order to find solitude, you should flee from a community. It is important to find God first in the community and trust that God will lead you into solitude. Although every silent moment remains the same, in true prayer every moment is a new discovery of a new silence, a new penetration into eternity in which all things are always new. The great work of the solitary life is gratitude.

Toward the end of his life, Thomas Merton received permission to become a hermit and move to a small cinderblock building in the woods, where his only companion was a black snake. Lying in a remote part of the monastery's two thousand acres this hidden bungalow, with its simple furnishings, provided a spiritual oasis where Merton could pray and write alone. The solitary life for Merton confirmed what he had learned from the desert fathers — that there would be temptations and joys, tears and "ineffable peace." There was, he felt, a purity about the happiness because it was not of his making but the gift of mercy. In the last analysis, what he was seeking in solitude was not fulfillment but salvation for all. Solitude, for Merton, is not separation:

> Some men have perhaps become hermits with the thought that sanctity could only be attained by escape from other men. But the only justification for a life of deliberate solitude is the conviction that it will help you to love not only God but also other men. If you go into the desert merely to get away from people you dislike, you will find neither peace nor solitude; you will only isolate yourself with a tribe of devils.
>   Man seeks unity because he is the image of the One God. Unity implies solitude, and hence the need to be physically alone. But unity and solitude are not metaphysical isolation. He who isolates himself in order to enjoy a kind of independence in his egotistical and external self does not find unity at all, for he disintegrates into a multiplicity of conflicting passions and finally ends in confusion and total unreality. Solitude is not and can never be a narcissistic dialogue of the ego with itself.[5]

Truth and Censorship

Through Merton's writings on solitude, people come in touch with their own authentic selves, according to Brother Patrick Hart, who worked as Merton's secretary. Brother Patrick edited some of Merton's books and was the general editor of Merton's journals, personally editing the first and seventh volumes. "I think he'd say to us today: 'Slow down, no matter what your way of life is or what your job is. You can find a time to be alone with God and in prayer.' That is what comes across to me in his writings. What Merton achieved, he did it in his own unique way. Only he and God know exactly how he managed it. It was a bit of a miracle, I think. He would just take off on a long walk in the woods in the morning and clear his mind, then come back, seem able to write and to know exactly what he was going to say. But he needed the time alone before he could enter into that activity.

"I would never bother him if I knew he was typing. He typed very fast, using his finger and his thumb. He was like a fan. We called it the biblical system — 'seek and find.' He would type as much with four fingers as I would with ten. I used to bring his meal over along with the reports from the censors. He'd say: 'If you quoted the Our Father, they'd expect you to do a footnote.' When his peace and justice writings were blocked by the abbot general, that was hard for him to take. He was writing against the American government and criticizing the use of nuclear weapons. The abbot general was a Gaulist and he defended France's right to develop their weapons. After the publication in April 1963 of *Pacem in Terris* [the papal encyclical on establishing universal peace through truth, justice, charity, and liberty] Merton wrote to the abbot general and said it was a good thing Pope John XXIII didn't have to pass the Trappist censorship or the document would never have got through. He seemed always to have the last word. He would do it in a humorous way, but he would always get his point across."

Merton strongly believed that military might could never defend true liberty that began inside people's souls. They would never be free so long as they harbored money, power, and comfort. He was also at pains to point out that those who opposed nuclear war were not necessarily enemies of America or paid agents of communism, as some thought at the time. "His views on Vietnam, Hiroshima, and Nagasaki never bothered me because I felt he knew what he was talking about," said Brother Patrick. "But I think there was an element in the community — conservatives, rather traditional people who liked the pure contemplative life without any agitation — who felt Merton was engaging in a little too much activity. Yet Merton felt very deeply that some people should speak out. The bishops were supposed to, he pointed out, but they weren't saying anything. Theologians were being very coy because, if they said anything, they would be told to move. If priests were intent on becoming bishops, they had to be very careful what they spoke about or they wouldn't get up the ladder, so there were always reasons. But Merton felt free of them as a monk. In his mind, he could speak out, which he did very effectively." As Merton wrote in his journal on March 3, 1964:

> I had been hoping to republish a few articles on nuclear war that had been permitted by Dom Gabriel — thinking that it was enough that he had permitted them once. Not so. The new General, Dom Ignace Gillet, dug into the files, held a meeting of Definitors, and declared that there was to be no republishing of these articles. Thus I am still not permitted to say what Pope John said in *Pacem in Terris*. Reason: "That is not the job of a monk, it is for the Bishops." Certainly it has a basis in the monastic tradition. "The job of the monk is to weep, not to teach." But with our cheese business and all the other "weeping" functions we have undertaken, it seems strange that a monk should be forbidden to stand up for the truth, particularly when the truth (in this case) is disastrously neglected.[6]

A Clash of Images

As you read Merton, it soon becomes apparent that his cultural critique can apply as much to the early part of the twenty-first century as it did to the middle years of the twentieth. This is why he can indubitably be claimed as a spiritual master for all seasons. Although he cites specific historical events, there is a timeless quality about his diagnosis because he is always pointing toward the eternal. He sees beyond and within "the world." A prophet for a news-dominated culture, Merton is the antithesis of a "news junkie," someone who monitors bulletins obsessively. He says he hardly ever watches television or reads papers, receiving his information largely through correspondence. Describing himself as a journalist because he is "one who observes," he can be nevertheless scathing toward mainstream journalistic activity. He condemns newspapers for manufacturing "pseudo-news" and dismisses the earnest scanning of newsprint as "the ritual morning trance," a plunge into so-called "reality" which is, as he sees it, an abomination of superstition and idolatry issuing from minds that are full of myths, distortions, half-truths, and evasions. He complains:

> Why can we not be content with the secret gift of the happiness that God offers us, without consulting the rest of the world? Why do we insist, rather, on a happiness that is approved by the magazines and TV? Perhaps because we do not believe in a happiness that is given to us for nothing. We do not think we can be happy with a happiness that has no price tag on it.[7]

Even in the 1960s, Merton considers the world to be in a profound spiritual crisis, evidenced by desperation, cynicism, violence, conflict, self-contradiction, ambivalence, fear and hope, doubt and belief, creation and destructiveness, progress and regression, along with an obsessive attachment to images, idols, and slogans, which only momentarily dulls the anguish before it breaks out somewhere else in more sinister guise. One can only imagine the force of his indictment of today's interactive kingdom of multiplatform communication. In his eyes, "the world" is "a complete and systematic sham," and people who follow its creed can only pretend they are alive. This is most notably the case with modern business practice:

> Businesses are, in reality, quasi-religious sects. When you go to work in one you embrace *a new faith*. And if they are really big businesses, you progress from faith to a kind of mystique. Belief in the product, preaching the product, in the end the product becomes the focus of a transcendental experience. Through "the product" one communes with the vast forces of life, nature, and history that are expressed in business. Why not face it? Advertising treats all products with the reverence and the seriousness due to sacraments.[8]

Such opinions opened Merton to criticism that a monk in an enclosed order could hardly understand the ethos of the business world in much the same way as the manager of a public relations firm could have little perception of the purpose of a Cistercian monastery. Perhaps Merton was harsh in his judgments because he felt the world had once contaminated him, and he had vowed never to fall prey again to its deceptions.

Merton was a personalist who believed that science and technology had their place in the realm of human improvement, so long as they respected that the origin and goal of all being lay in God. He spoke about the divine image in all people and about the ordinariness of contemplation, noting that the dehumanizing effects of technology could easily lead to cultural disintegration. Every person, he believed, was theomorphic (God-shaped) and essentially contemplative. Merton's critique of technocratic society was based on its effect on the human person. He came to see the monk as a social critic who operated from the fringes of society, mirroring the early desert tradition with its rejection of compromise and convention. To be a contemplative was to be an outlaw.

Assassination and Sacrifice

The prophetic nature of monastic living meant witnessing, not only to intellectual truth, but also to what he called "mystic truth," the integral truth of life, history, humanity, and God. His visionary stance on issues of civil rights and social justice had been kindled in the summer of 1941 when he worked briefly in Harlem at Friendship House, a movement founded by the Catholic social justice activist Catherine de Hueck Doherty, one of the leading proponents of interracial justice before the days of Martin Luther King Jr. Merton later read King's *Stride toward Freedom* about the first major campaign of the civil rights movement, the Montgomery bus boycott, and sensed its Christian character. He was moved and disturbed by John Howard Griffin's memoir, *Black Like Me,* an account of dyeing his skin and traveling to the South. He also read books by the civil rights advocate James Baldwin, who argued that the liberation of blacks was necessary for the liberation of whites.

Little could be expected of white liberals who sympathized but did
nothing. Merton saw that the movement for racial justice was an
expression of *kairos,* a time of crisis and opportunity that called for
a radical change of heart and direction. Integration could not merely
mean the inclusion of blacks into an otherwise unchanged social
structure but a renewal of the basic human values of liberty and
community. Black Muslims who, he observed, had ceased to look
upon anything in the world as funny, formed one of the few fanat-
ical movements for which he had respect and which they deserved
because they had transformed the lives of "wrecks, criminals, men
in despair." Merton writes:

> Martin Luther King, who is no fanatic but a true Christian,
> writes a damning letter from Birmingham jail, saying that the
> churches have utterly failed the Negro. In the end, that is what
> the Black Muslims are saying too. And there is truth in it. Not
> that there is not a certain amount of liberal and sincere con-
> cern for civil rights among Christians, even among ministers,
> priests, and bishops. But what is this sincerity worth? What
> does this "good will" amount to? Is it anything more than a
> spiritual luxury, to calm the conscience of those who cultivate
> it? What good does it do the Negro? What good does it do
> the country? Is it a pure evasion of reality?[9]

King and other civil rights leaders had planned to make a retreat at
Gethsemani in the spring of 1968. Canon A. M. (Donald) Allchin,
a distinguished Anglican scholar, recalled the day he and Merton
drove to Shakertown at Pleasant Hill in Kentucky in the pouring
rain. On the return journey they heard on the car radio that King
had been assassinated in Memphis. "Merton seemed utterly hit by
it, but it was as if he had known the assassination might happen,"
said Allchin. "The atmosphere in the car became absolutely silent.
He asked if we could pull into a siding where we stayed quietly
for about a quarter of an hour. The light was fading, but Merton
said we could not go straight back to the monastery. We had to go
to Bardstown, where there was a small restaurant, Colonel Hawk's

Diner, owned by a black American Catholic whom Merton knew. Merton felt Hawk would be devastated by the news and, because two of his teenage children were away at college, might be anxious about possible race riots. "Merton wanted to express his total solidarity with the man, and Hawk gave us a table by ourselves on one side of the restaurant. Hawk wanted to talk to us and, although he must have been devastated inside, I suddenly realized this was the first time that I had had a serious conversation with a black American. There was something wonderful about the man, even though he must have been feeling terrible. The following morning I attended a Mass of the Sorrows of Mary, which Merton said in a small chapel on behalf of Coretta, who had helped lead the American civil rights movement.

"Everything that moves Barack Obama moved Merton, who was very conscious of racial issues. I should be very surprised if Obama has not read Merton. He is very fierce on some of the same issues Merton would have been fierce about. As we get further from Merton in time, we get nearer to him in thought because he was so far ahead of his own time that we haven't caught up with him yet. Merton and Obama are both universal men in a special way and they both belong to the future."

Some claim that Merton's essays on Christian nonviolence went beyond anything written by Martin Luther King Jr. or Mahatma Gandhi. Merton is believed to have been the first Roman Catholic to join the Protestant Fellowship of Reconciliation, and later he helped found the Catholic Peace Fellowship, the precursor to Pax Christi in the United States, part of the international peace movement. Merton argued that prayer and sacrifice were the most effective spiritual weapons in the war against war and had to be used with deliberate aim: not for a nebulous hope of peace and security but directly against any form of violence and war. This meant that people should be willing to sacrifice and restrain their own instincts for violence and aggression in their relationship with others. Merton writes:

> We may never succeed in this campaign, but whether we succeed or not the duty is evident. It is the great Christian task of

our time. Everything else is secondary, for the survival of the human race depends upon it. We must at least face this responsibility and do something about it. And the first job of all is to understand the psychological forces at work in ourselves and in society.[10]

Merton praised Gandhi as a model of integrity who could not be ignored. A Hindu who had applied Christian values to social problems, he had developed a style that was both political and religious at the same time. Merton aligned himself with the nonviolent principles of Gandhi because they sought truth, not power. In "A Tribute to Gandhi," Merton states that Gandhi emphasized the importance of the individual person entering political action "with a fully awakened and operative spiritual power in himself, the power of *satyagraha,* nonviolent dedication to truth, a religious and spiritual force, a wisdom born of fasting and prayer."[11] Those who viewed this as "enthusiasm" or "fanaticism" made a "lamentable mistake," estranging those who had found refuge in "groups dominated by a confused pseudo-spirituality or by totalitarian messianism."[12] He continues: "Gandhi's religio-political action was based on an ancient metaphysic of man, a philosophical wisdom which is common to Hinduism, Buddhism, Islam, Judaism, and Christianity: that 'truth is the inner law of our being.'"[13]

Zen, Beer, and Jazz

On my tour of Gethsemani, I came to an enclosed area where Merton had once constructed a Zen garden as a place of peaceful meditation for fully professed monks. Every Easter Morning, a two-foot long orange fish kite would be suspended on a pole so that its large, wide mouth could catch the wind and float around in the breeze. The graveled garden conveyed a stark beauty and featured an eye-catching piece of limestone that looked like dark, porous moon rock. Merton always desired to bring together the basic principles of monasticism within religious traditions. In fact, he saw them as already united. Just as there was a continuity between the Eastern and Western forms of monasticism, an underlying bridge that had not been crossed, so the simplicity of Cistercian architecture was, in a sense, a continuation of the Zen form. "Zen" (which Merton saw as an important instrument in his apostolate) derives from the Chinese word *Ch'an,* meaning meditation. Merton comes close to an understanding of Zen when he describes contemplation as "life itself, fully awake, fully active, fully aware that it is alive."[14] Zen is a realization rather than a doctrine, a disciplined way of being present, of stilling and silencing the mind from mental distractions and suffering. It is not a religion, philosophy, method, or system but an ontological awareness of pure being beyond subject and object, an immediate grasp of being in its "suchness" and "thusness." It is not an "awareness of" anything but pure awareness itself. But its characteristics of self-analysis, self-reflection, and self-discovery do not mean isolation from communion with other people. To follow the way of Zen is not about closing oneself off from people in the world but about becoming more open and compassionate toward them. *No Man Is an Island* is not only the title of one of Merton's books but also a fundamental concept in Zen thinking.

After dismissing oriental mysticism in his younger years, he had come to appreciate the importance of experience over verbal formulations and was attracted by the writings of Daisetz Suzuki, the noted Buddhist monk and Japanese Zen scholar regarded as the foremost interpreter of Zen in the West. They exchanged extensive correspondence for several years and, in June 1964, Merton returned to New York City for the first time in twenty-three years to meet him. Suzuki told Merton that his book *Ascent to Truth* was popular among Zen scholars and monks. Merton was not interested in purely abstract metaphysical systems but in *intuition.* He discerned something close to Zen within Christian metaphysical and mystical experience. Merton's pamphlet *The Zen Revival,* published by the Buddhist Society of London, was sold and promoted by members as the most reliable expression of Zen, and, in one of his letters,

Merton said he felt he understood Zen Buddhists more than Roman Catholics.

Jazz percussionist and meditation teacher Richard Sisto was a member of a marginal group of poets, musicians, and artists with whom Merton felt a particular affinity because, like monks, their lives were a contradiction of, and an enigma to, functional, materialistic culture. Merton would practice Eastern forms of meditation with them. A leading vibraphonist, who has recorded with some of the biggest names in jazz, Richard Sisto describes himself as "a Christian, Buddhist, Hindu (Advaita Yoga) practitioner." He told me how he had moved to Louisville and played at 118 Washington, a jazz club where Merton occasionally turned up. "The owner turned to me on a break one evening and said 'that monk was in here again.' Soon after I met Merton through a priest friend, I would visit him at Gethsemani, usually on one of the lakes, drinking beer and talking about God and Zen. He was engaging and totally present to you if the conversation and the topic were genuine and timely. When the talk was over, he could be abrupt, another quality I admired and shared. I was reading most of his works at the time, and he gave me a few unpublished documents that have since been printed. I was raised a Catholic and attended the seminary in Chicago for a couple of years so it was easy to resonate with him, moving from the Christian mystics to the Zen masters and yogis. He made everything we were into at the time become more significant. His encouragement and approval of our direction was amazing. I have had a dream about him that confirms him as one of my true spiritual teachers. I often quote him to my meditation students. His loving openness and great enthusiasm for the spiritual path is something that will remain with me forever."

One of the most helpful pieces of advice Merton gave Richard Sisto was about the need to avoid "the larger context" where the possibility for success might be greater, in favor of a smaller place where he would have more time to think and pray. Richard followed his guidance and later went to live with his wife, Penny, on a farm adjoining Gethsemani, where they raised nine children. One of them is the television and film actor Jeremy Sisto, who played Billy Chenowith in the HBO series *Six Feet Under* and took the lead in the NBC and TNT miniseries *Jesus and Julius Caesar.* He was, in fact, baptized "Jeremy Merton" in honor of his father's friendship with the monk and has read some of Merton's books, discerning within the writings a prophetic wisdom for the twenty-first century.

A Communion of Love

Merton's intense study of the Christian mystical tradition, through such figures as the desert fathers, Pseudo-Dionysius, St. Bernard of Clairvaux, Meister Eckhart, and St. John of the Cross, grounded him in the spirituality of his own faith tradition while providing him with the freedom to connect more meaningfully with the wisdom of the East. His knowledge of the Western mystics enabled him to enter into dialogue with representatives of Eastern religious traditions. Increasingly, Merton came to value experience over speculative theology and the inadequacy of words to express any form of religious experience. Perceiving the unity of all reality, he saw that the goal of all spiritual discipline was a transformation of consciousness, but to achieve it, you had to be liberated from attachments. Just as Greek philosophy and Roman law had contributed to the formation of Christian culture, so Western Christian thought would have been "immeasurably enriched and deepened," he felt, by an openness to Eastern philosophy. The Asian heritage was far more than a theme in the study of comparative religion or a rival system to refute. Merton writes:

> Wisdom is not penetrated by logical analysis. The values hidden in Oriental thought actually reveal themselves only on the plane of spiritual experience, or perhaps, if you like, of aesthetic experience. They belong, of course, to the natural order: but they certainly have deep affinities with supernatural wisdom itself. Surely we cannot doubt that they may be able, if properly grasped and appreciated, to lead us to a deeper

and wiser understanding of our own magnificent mystical tradition, just as Platonism, without actually "influencing" the
Greek Fathers, gave them a language and a sensibility that
were equipped to penetrate in a specially significant way the
depths of the revealed mystery of Christ.

At least this much can and must be said: the "universality"
and "catholicity" which are essential to the Church necessarily
imply an ability and a readiness to enter into dialogue with
all that is pure, wise, profound, and humane in every kind
of culture. In this one sense at least a dialogue with Oriental
wisdom becomes necessary. A Christian culture that is not
capable of such a dialogue would show, by that very fact, that
it lacked catholicity.[15]

In Merton's eyes, genuine dialogue should end not in communication but in communion — a joining of hearts, but with each person
remaining faithful to his or her own religious search. The essential
monastic experience is centered always on Love. There is only one
thing to live for and that is Love. This is another reason why Merton
is a prophetic voice for the interreligious world of today. The Dalai
Lama, who met Merton during his Asian pilgrimage, said Merton
had introduced him to the real meaning of the word "Christian"
and that Buddhist monks and nuns could learn much about the
practical implications of compassion through Christianity's record
of charitable work, especially in schools and hospitals. "When you
see the photograph of Merton with the Dalai Lama, they look like
two cats who've licked up all the cream," smiled Donald Allchin.
"The whole relationship between the Tibetan monastic world and
Christianity altered on that day and it has been altering ever since."
    In his last few weeks, Merton visited the stone-carved statues
of seated and reclining Buddhas at Polonnaruwa in Ceylon (now
Sri Lanka). It was a profound spiritual awakening. He could not
write about the experience hastily and, even when he managed
to, considered the words an inadequate expression of what had
happened:

I am able to approach the Buddhas barefoot and undisturbed, my feet in wet grass, wet sand. Then the silence of the extraordinary faces. The great smiles. Huge and yet subtle. . . . Looking at these figures I was suddenly, almost forcibly, jerked clean out of the habitual, half-tied vision of things, and an inner clearness, clarity, as if exploding from the rocks themselves, became evident and obvious. The queer *evidence* of the reclining figure, the smile, the sad smile of Ananda standing with arms folded (much more "imperative" than da Vinci's *Mona Lisa* because completely simple and straightforward). The thing about all this is that there is no puzzle, no problem, and really no "mystery." All problems are resolved and everything is clear, simply because what matters is clear. The rock, all matter, all life, is charged with dharmakaya . . . everything is emptiness and everything is compassion. I don't know when in my life I have ever had such a sense of beauty and spiritual validity running together in one aesthetic illumination.[16]

The Higher Ground

Six days later, after addressing a conference in Thailand, Merton died unexpectedly at the age of fifty-three. He was electrocuted by a faulty fan in his room at a complex in the suburbs of Bangkok. Ironically, the body of the internationally renowned peace writer was brought back to America in a plane that also bore the corpses of U.S. soldiers killed in Vietnam. It was an extraordinary and paradoxical culmination to a life that had been replete with its own extraordinary paradoxes. But as a pioneer of interfaith dialogue, he was never a syncretist and knew the limits of ecumenism. Fundamentally, what he learned from other religions improved his understanding of his own tradition. Merton represented the beginning of an era in which the quest for the integration of the contemplative and the prophetic, between mysticism and politics, was viewed as an increasingly central dimension of Christian life. A transitional figure in relation to the shift from one phase of Catholic culture to another, he was always marginal, influencing the world far beyond the confines of institutional Christianity and building bridges with sections of community largely ignored by the white male clerics of the day. He was a social critic who provided theological and spiritual nourishment for people in the midst of struggle.

In the fortieth anniversary year of Merton's death, at St. Peter's Catholic Church in Big Pine Key, Florida, I met Joan Carter McDonald, who worked at the Pentagon for ten years, from the time of the Cuban missile crisis in 1962. Involved in civilian employment issues related to the Vietnam War, she later served in senior management positions at two government agencies in Washington, DC. A lifelong reader of Merton, she wrote a personal biography of the monk, which was published in 2006.[17] McDonald's work with the federal government provided particular insights into the furor over Merton's outspoken judgments on foreign affairs. In his diary, Merton attributed his official silencing on writing about war and peace to be the result of U.S. government influence on church superiors.

"Merton could be a voice for any leader to call for a moral imperative in these times," said Joan McDonald. "Like President Obama, Merton believed in speaking out and seeking support from the people to direct government action in the best interests of the general public. Human respect and observance of human rights take priority over petty greed, self-interest, and self-indulgence. Merton spoke of general moral principles and did not resort to reliance on enforcement of specific doctrine to persuade people to his point of view. He sought a higher ground — the principle of human dignity in the process of governance, protecting the rights of all peoples in the equality of creation."

Joan McDonald cited an undated letter by Merton to an unnamed "statesman's wife" in which he had written:

> We are living in a dream world. We do not know ourselves or our adversaries. We are myths to ourselves and they are myths to us. And we are secretly persuaded that we can shoot it out like the sheriffs and cattle rustlers on TV. This is not reality

and the President can do a tremendous amount to get people to see the fact, more than any single person. If he can get the country to face reality and accept it and try to cope with it on a sober basis, without expecting miracles at every turn, we may begin to get ourselves together. But for this one has to have motives and principles, and that is just what too many people have thrown overboard.[18]

Comparisons continue to be drawn between the vision of Barack Obama and Thomas Merton. "I'd be loath to tie Merton down to one or two presidential terms," said Dr. Paul Pearson, director and archivist of the Thomas Merton Center at Bellarmine University, Louisville. "I think Merton's message will speak for a long time as it is firmly rooted in the best of the Christian tradition. The issues he was writing about in the sixties are just as relevant today as then. In recent years he seems to have been of particular interest to the former Eastern bloc countries, and there has also been a growing interest in Asia. The Dalai Lama summed Merton up well on one of his visits to Gethsemani when he said: 'As for myself, I always consider myself as one of his Buddhist brothers. So as a close friend — or as his brother — I always remember him, and I always admire his activities and his lifestyle. Since my meeting with him, and so often when I examine myself, I really follow some of his examples.... And so for the rest of my life, the impact of meeting him will remain until my last breath. I really want to state that I make this commitment, and this will remain until my last breath.' "

Hailed as the greatest spiritual writer and spiritual master of the twentieth century in English-speaking America, Merton continues to be one of the most widely read religious authors in the world. No other person has had such a profound influence in the spiritual sphere as Merton. All the more surprising, perhaps, that when the American bishops included biographical sketches of prominent American Catholics in their new catechism for young people, they excluded Thomas Merton, allegedly because of his affiliation with the other great religions. While such an oversight might have been the sour fruit of fear (for Merton was a dangerous thinker), it seems indefensible that his name should have been omitted. However, as Paul Pearson pointed out, Merton himself would probably have been relieved in much the same way as he objected to being turned into "a Catholic myth for children in parochial schools." Although Merton never regarded himself as a papist, his position was in line with the thinking of the Second Vatican Council, as well as the biblical prophetic tradition. His witness was recognized by both Pope John XXIII and Paul VI. Pope John XXIII's personal gift to Merton was the stole he had worn for his enthronement, while Pope Paul VI presented Merton with a crucifix.

It has to be said, though, that Merton saw himself as belonging to the world and not just the Roman Catholic Church, which at times he felt could be a manifestation of both spiritual sickness and inexpressible life. In a letter to a fellow priest in 1967, he acknowledges that there is much within institutions that is unhealthy and false: "Submission is canonized and all opposition is suspect. There is a machinery that grinds everyone to powder. Then, as you say, the effect is that when we finally open our mouths we are so wrought up that we explode, and that, too, is held against us."[19]

In assessing Merton's influence, Paul Pearson said that, during one week in 2009, he had worked with researchers or publishers from Sweden, Poland, Chile, Ukraine, England, Ireland, Korea, Australia, the United States, and Canada — a cross-section that was not untypical. The broad areas of interest reflected Merton's own. The Merton Collection at Bellarmine was started by Merton in 1963 and, four years later he made it the official repository. It has grown to far in excess of fifty thousand items, including Merton's original manuscripts, photographs, recordings, and calligraphies. There are more than twenty thousand pieces of correspondence to over twenty-one hundred correspondents as well as a large collection of academic materials about the writer, including three hundred doctoral and master's theses and other dissertations. The center receives up to three thousand visitors a year.

Through this study and writing, Merton went back to the great sources of the Christian Catholic tradition and reinterpreted them for the modern world. He made them available to a readership that would not otherwise have had had access to them. But as a writer he felt compelled to address the pressing issues of his day from his perspective within the monastic tradition. "Merton's understanding of the Christian tradition of spirituality introduced many to the contemplative dimension of spiritual living," said Dr. Pearson. "It led Merton to take a prophetic stance with regard to many of the issues facing humankind, issues as pressing today as when Merton wrote about them over forty years ago. This shaped his approach to ecumenical and interfaith dialogue taking place on the experiential and not solely the doctrinal level. It also influenced monastic life and his leadership of monastic reform. It is extraordinary how one man could accomplish so much in just twenty years' work. *The Seven Storey Mountain* was published in 1948 and he was dead in 1968. He was certainly a genius."

While the power of Merton continues to touch and stir people in many different realms, he did not publish any manifesto or claim any official authority for his views. His brilliance lay in the fact that he was an honest searcher for the truth who empowered others in the process. The Reverend Canon David Scott, an Anglican priest in Winchester, in the south of England, was originally drawn to Merton after spotting, on the shelves of his local public library, a picture of a monk with a shaven head, tonsured in white robes, meditating high up in a forest. He was attracted by Merton's freedom to be a contemplative, while remaining sociable, humorous, and human. "He managed to be truly human, yet profoundly in touch with the Divine," said Canon Scott. "Merton discovered the humanity of God as the potential divine nature of all human beings. The secret is no secret at all. It is every human being's birthright to find themselves at home with God.

"I would rate his contribution to ecumenism highly. He had a large circle of friends and correspondents all over the world.

Eventually he invited local ministers into his hermitage for ecumenical sharing, particularly the Baptists. Perhaps he was least sympathetic to his own Roman Catholic Church, feeling he was able to be critical about something he knew a lot about. Merton had deep roots in his own Catholic orders but, being so secure in his sense of belonging to God, he clung very lightly to the rules. The Spirit was more important.

"I have valued Merton's big heart in my pastoral ministry and the prayer through it all. Merton has encouraged me to be a poet in the church — to follow the gifts one has and to draw into the Eucharist, like Teilhard de Chardin, the whole world. It is about being open to the natural world and praying in the Eucharist for its welfare against the onslaught of the modern gods of progress. Merton knew that the contemplative monastic life was for him. He reshaped it like St. Bernard did before him. He was monk, a *monos,* a one-off in God's eyes, and he flourished in that environment. He loved it enough to hate it at times. But God 'did it' for him."

When he began life as a monk, Thomas Merton thought he knew all the answers. But as he grew older and spent longer in solitude, he felt he had only just begun to seek the questions. As he explored the inner terrain and moved beyond explanations, he found he could speak more hopefully through experience, offering heart and encouragement to the world, a reassurance that is certainly needed today.

The message of hope the contemplative offers you ... is not that you need to find your way through the jungle of language and problems that today surround God: but that whether you understand or not, God loves you, is present to you, lives in you, dwells in you, calls you, saves you, and offers you an understanding and light which are like nothing you ever found in books or heard in sermons. The contemplative has nothing to tell you except to reassure you and say that, if you dare to penetrate your own silence and risk the sharing of that solitude with the lonely other who seeks God through you, then you will truly recover the light and the capacity to understand what is beyond words and beyond explanations because it is too close to be explained: it is the intimate union in the depths of your own heart, of God's Spirit and your own secret inmost self, so that you and He are in all truth One Spirit.[20]

TWO

The Monk and the Archbishop

A Conversation about Merton
with Dr. Rowan Williams

"Every time I read Merton, I have a renewed sense that this is the world I want to inhabit," said the Archbishop of Canterbury, Dr. Rowan Williams, sitting in his spacious study at Lambeth Palace, beside the River Thames in London.

"I think Merton has given me a sense of the largeness of the classical Christian world — that world of the monastic fathers, to some extent the medieval world at its best, and that openness to other traditions East and West. I think it is the feeling that that classical Christian world of doctrinal vision is big enough for far more than a lot of people think. It is hugely deep and resilient, capable of engaging intelligently and compassionately with political reality and other faiths."

The archbishop's room (book lined and icon laden) looks out onto lawns and trees, a peaceful landscape for a peace-loving man. While he works at his desk on speeches and homilies, a framed photograph of Thomas Merton is propped to one side. Occasional glances into the contemplative's eyes provide brotherly inspiration and support as Dr. Williams wrestles with his responsibilities as spiritual head of the Anglican Communion. There is also a copy of a watercolor featuring Canterbury Cathedral, painted by Merton's artist father, Owen. It was presented to the archbishop by the Thomas Merton Society of Great Britain and Ireland after a talk he gave on the fortieth anniversary of Merton's death.

Rowan Williams told me that he felt Thomas Merton was very much a man for the times. He was not infallible, not a guru, and not always right. In fact, he was "a very complicated human being indeed." Yet "going back to him, I find again and again that things he wrote in 1962 or 1967 could have been written yesterday. I even discovered, extraordinarily, a little passage in his journals where he mentions Guantánamo Bay, purely coincidentally you might say. But he's writing about the Americans clinging on to bits of Cuban territory. He refers to Guantánamo Bay and how that is a sign of all the things that go wrong in international relations. It suddenly sprang off the page three or four years ago when I was reading for a paper I was writing about Merton's theological politics in this period."

Diagnosis and Projection

Dr. Williams said he believed that *Conjectures of a Guilty Bystander,* the monk's musings on the world in the early 1960s, had a particular relevance for our age. "I have been back to *Conjectures* several times in the last couple of years, looking at some of its ideas about prayer and contemplation, liturgy, the environment, and about peace and war. It is extraordinarily pertinent. In that period Merton was, I think, asking himself deep questions about what a healthy society and a sick society look like. He knew he was inhabiting a very sick society in many ways and his diagnosis of that — the acquisitiveness, the rape of the earth, racism, the militarism — is as relevant now as it was then.

"I think Obama's election is in some ways a sign of American society's willingness to turn away from some of the sicknesses Merton identified with. We'll see how it turns out, but there's an element of it there. Merton was, I think, in some ways very naïve about politics, and I think perhaps did not really engage with how very difficult it is for decision makers to change a political climate. But at least in the diagnosis — "what do we need as a society?" — he's very sharp and very creative in his way. I'd like to see that voice around the new regime. "In *Conjectures,* Merton is very aware of society's scapegoating instinct. It would be fascinating to put him along side someone like René Girard in analysis there but he does have that sense that we consistently deal with our problems by projection.[1] He comments fascinatingly in *Conjectures* that the profound and violent anti-Semitism of the early Middle Ages in the Western church went with a kind of adoption of an Old Testament view of what the church was — the church identifying itself as the chosen people of God, on the march, heavily armed. He uses that as a way of saying that we project onto others the unacceptable image that we are, in fact, inhabiting ourselves. We see in others the unacceptable face of what we are. There is a great deal there for us to think about. All that he wrote about the Cold War is connected with that kind of analysis of displacement, scapegoating, projection, and the 'mimetic quality of violence,' to quote Girard. We are violent because we learn violence from the other and we go on mirroring that backward and forward to infinity if we are not broken out of it."

"Amazing Hospitality"

The archbishop said that, for Thomas Merton, faith was "far, far deeper" than simply adopting a certain set of views that could lead you into yet another kind of tribalism. It was profoundly an encounter with "the unmasterable, the unmanageable, the unspeak-able, or with that which cannot be spoken of." That was why his poetry was important. "I think what he is seeking, especially in the 1960s, is how to be an orthodox but nontribal catholic, how to get inside the language of doctrine so that you understand what it's about. His early book *The New Man,* which he didn't think much of in his later years, lays out, in fact, quite a good and system-atic picture of how Christian doctrine — about Creation, Fall and Redemption, the Holy Spirit — can be understood as this tremen-dously profound opening to the mysterious. Allegiance to Christ within that is not nailing your colors to yet another tribal mast but actually understanding that there is humanity: there is the full space and scope of being human.

"What I find very interesting in his writing of the early to mid-1960s is that there is often an impatience with some of the Vatican II radicalism coming through because it is just rootless. What's the point of giving up plainsong? Does that actually help us at all in understanding and inhabiting the world that God wants us to inhabit? Well, no it doesn't. What you are doing actually is replacing one kind of tradition, which may be a bit fossilized, with another set of conventions which don't have anything like the depth to explore."

Born in Swansea, South Wales, in 1950, Rowan Williams started reading Merton when he was eighteen, the year the monk died. He said he was initially drawn to the writings "a little bit by the lure of the exotic." It had been simply fascinating to read the journals of an enclosed monk. *The Sign of Jonas* was one of the first books by Merton to catch his attention. Then, before going up to university at Cambridge, Williams read *Elected Silence*, the abridged version of *The Seven Storey Mountain*. But the book that had "most struck me and most held me — and still does" was *Conjectures of a Guilty Bystander*. "That was such a crucial period for him and for the church. To me, reading it as an eighteen-year-old, it was a kind of distillation of what was best, both in the tradition and in the new Vatican II world. It was a book of amazing hospitality. He writes about the Swiss Protestant theologian Karl Barth, the German-Jewish political theorist Hannah Arendt, the Russian theologian Paul Evdokimov, and about the poets he's encountered. You have that sense of a mind really at its highest pitch, entertaining all these remarkable spiritual and intellectual guests, and working over what they were saying. That attracted me hugely."

As the years passed, Rowan Williams found himself studying Merton compulsively — "he fits very well with your teens and twenties." He was absorbed by what the author wrote about silence and solitude because of Merton's sense that you go into silence in order, not to cut things out, but to enter into the questions you might otherwise be avoiding. "One of the themes that comes up again and again, especially in Merton's writing of late 1950s–early 1960s, is that you become a monk or a solitary to face yourself," he said. "So, far from being an evasive turn, it's all about coming to terms with a lot most people don't want to see. Therefore solitude is the deepest kind of connection, a familiar paradox. I think what he is saying here is that we all need to be quiet enough to be subject to our own scrutiny. For Christian and non-Christian alike, this is an absolute lifeline of sanity in a world which often encourages us not to face what we don't want to look at in ourselves and so gives us endless distractions to prevent that happening."

Reading Merton these days, the archbishop realized how difficult it had actually been for Merton to find silence and solitude. The silent monk had been a compulsive communicator. "I just cannot get my mind around the quantity of words that he poured out. One of the nicest bits in the correspondence is with a teenager in California, Suzanne Butorovich, who writes to him at one point: 'I looked you up in the school library catalogue and, good grief, why do you write so much?' It was a real paradox, but the diagnosis remains very clear. He knows what the problems are. I think it's that honesty which is disarming in him as well. It's not just the enthusiasm with which he embraces the new stimuli but the honesty."

Returning to the Sources

The archbishop's affinity with the Orthodox spiritual tradition had clearly been enriched by his reading of Merton. Some of the theologians who "had really kept Merton going" in his early monastic life — and some of those who had got him there in the first place — had been part of a remarkable generation of French theologians in the 1940s. Men like Jean Daniélou were returning to the sources. *Ressourcement* was the movement that saw the key to the revitalization of theology and pastoral life in the church as lying in a reappropriation of the sources. That period saw the publication of an acclaimed series of early Christian works in French translation, Sources Chrétiennes, and the writings of Henri de Lubac.

"Merton is formed by that in a sense, going back beyond Reformation controversies and the slightly sclerotic versions of religious life that developed in the eighteenth and nineteenth centuries, back to the sources, the desert fathers, the Eastern fathers. He certainly got from the Eastern fathers that sense of the dignity of the divine image in human beings, which is a fundamental theological point. That's all there in people like Daniélou. It comes through to Merton, who knew Daniélou and corresponded with him quite a bit:

> Fr. [Jean] Daniélou was here earlier in the summer. He is my director more or less. I need someone who can keep me straight in dealing with Oriental philosophies, and ecumenism. He is one of the best, and a charming person. I have always liked him.[2]

"Then he encounters again," explained Rowan Williams, "a modern Eastern Orthodox voice and finds it deeply, deeply sympathetic. So what he writes in *Conjectures* about Paul Evdokimov is very, very significant in the development of his own thinking. Evdokimov's work on what it is to be living out a monastic vocation as an ordinary human being really triggers something very deep in Merton":

> Evdokimov demands a virile ascesis, not simply gentlemanly retirement into leisure. The monk does not build his monastic city "on the margin" of the world but *instead of it*. This is important. The monastic consciousness of today in America is simply a marginal worldly consciousness. It won't do. On the other hand, I do not think the crumbling lavras and sketes of Athos will do much better.
>
> For Father Evdokimov, the monastic life is there to proclaim the abolition of history. How many Western monks could swallow that? Few, I imagine. Yet I see what he means.

He aims this statement shrewdly against the activistic, care-worn, busy-busy preoccupation of monks with ephemeral projects that have no deep significance. He has nothing to do whatever with the facile optimism of beatified agitation. His view of the Church and the world: since the world presents a *lying* vision, the unwordliness of the monk must be not only nonconformist, but provocatively so. The monk is *in revolt* against the false claims of the world. This has to be properly understood. There are enough emotionally disturbed people around who ask nothing better than to be dendrites and column sitters, to prove they are right and everyone else is wrong. Yet the principle is true.

I profoundly agree that in fact the monastic turning away from the world leads the monk, naturally, into a kind of prehistoric condition. Hence we are foolish to be too excited about playing an imaginary part, as monks in "history." But nevertheless, we are in history, not prehistory. (One might ask the question whether we will shortly be in posthistory.)[3]

Dr. Williams said that, as leader of the Anglican Communion, he often found himself leafing through Merton's books to help him reflect on the nature of prayer or to illustrate a spiritual point for a sermon. When preaching at ordinations, for instance, he liked to quote the spiritual master's own reflections on entering the priesthood:

My priestly ordination was, I felt, the one great secret for which I had been born. Ten years before I was ordained, when I was in the world, and seemed to be one of the men in the world most unlikely to become a priest, I had suddenly realized that for me ordination to the priesthood was, in fact, a matter of life or death, heaven or hell. As I finally came within sight of this perfect meeting with the inscrutable will of God, my vocation became clear. It was a mercy and a secret which were so purely mine that at first I intended to speak of them to no one.

Yet because no man is ordained priest for himself alone, and since my priesthood made me belong not only to God but also to all men, it was fitting that I should have spoken a little of what was in my heart to my friends who came to my ordination.[4]

The archbishop felt that *communion* had been a highly significant word and concept in Thomas Merton's spiritual syntax. Merton had loved the informal exchanges with people of other traditions, whether they were other Christians or people of other faiths. His *Asian Journal* remained, in many ways, "a great testament to communion":

I believe that by openness to Buddhism, to Hinduism, and to these great Asian traditions, we stand a wonderful chance of learning more about the potentiality of our own traditions, because they have gone, from the natural point of view, so much deeper into this than we have. The combination of the natural techniques and the graces and the other things that have been manifested in Asia and the Christian liberty of the gospel should bring us all at last to that full and transcendent liberty which is beyond mere cultural differences and mere externals — and mere this or that.[5]

Merton was clearly bored with official ecumenism and "not at all a man of the lowest common denominator." So the idea of communion had been pivotal to his thinking. "He had a huge confidence in the human instinct towards communion, and the sort of warning I suspect he wants to give to institutions is that all institutions tend to be controlled by anxiety sooner or later. While he himself is quite an anxious man in many ways, he knows that anxiety is not good for you. He wants to say to the institution, whether it's the monastery, the Catholic Church, or the Christian family of churches: 'Don't panic: trust God and God's image in human beings and you would be amazed what you get.' "

Compulsive and Elusive

Rowan Williams admitted that he thought, theoretically, Merton was "all over the place" because he was discovering things little by little: "He plunges in, splashes around, finds fascinating ideas, works on them, and corresponds." There was not a systematic theology of interfaith encounter in Merton's writings. That had not been his goal. Merton had been trying to express where he was and who he was to people in other religious traditions in a language he knew they could hear. Dr. Williams cited, as an example, Merton's correspondence in the 1960s with the Pakistani Muslim and Sufi scholar Abdul Aziz. At a time when there was no significant conversation between Muslims and Christians, they had managed to meet on the common ground of their religious experience. "You see that painstaking effort by Merton to speak Christianly in language that a Muslim can hear," said Dr. Williams. "That's a wonderful example for interfaith dialogue: Don't forget who you are and what language it is you speak. But ask yourself again and again how is it being heard?" There is certainly a contemporary tone to the words of Merton to Aziz on November 7, 1965:

> Well, my friend, we live in a troubled and sad time, and we must pray the infinite and merciful Lord to bear patiently with the sins of this world, which are very great. We must humble our hearts in silence and poverty of spirit and listen to His commands, which come from the depths of His love, and work that men's hearts may be converted to the ways of love and justice, not blood and murder, lust and greed. I am afraid that the big powerful countries are a very bad example to the rest of the world in this respect.[6]

But one of the hardest of Merton's journals to read, according to Dr. Williams, was *Learning to Love,* which gives an account of Merton's falling in love with a young nurse. "When I first read it, page after page, I kept thinking: 'For goodness sake, this is awful self-deceiving and self-justifying rhetoric. You are not saying what's going on.' Then I turned the page and found him saying: 'This is an awful self-deceiving rhetoric. I don't see what's going on.' He's always questioning and coming back to it. It's painful reading because it must have been a horrifically painful experience for everybody involved, but he doesn't lie about it or, if he does, he recognizes he's done it.

"He's a very mysterious person, the man nobody knows who has that strange recurring theme of disappearing. He talks about "disappearing into the Mass" when he is ordained, and of course almost his last recorded words are "So I will disappear," which was just a colloquial way of saying, "I'm off now." But there is that elusiveness about him, and his own sense of how he is a mystery to himself comes through very clearly. There is also the compulsive writing, journaling, letter writing as he tries to fathom a bit more about himself."

The Archbishop of Canterbury said that, while he had not read Thomas Merton so often when he was in his thirties and early forties, when he returned to him later in life, it was with the sense that the monastic writer continued to set a "standard of imaginative courage, coming out of deep prayerfulness."

THREE

Trusting the Heart

The Dynamics of Henri J. M. Nouwen

Even after many years of education and formation, even after the good advice and counsel of many, I can still say with Dante, "In the middle of the way of our life I find myself in a dark wood." This experience is frightful as well as exhilarating because it is the great experience of being alone, alone in the world, alone before God.[1]

"I'm not a very harmonious person who has everything in balance," admitted the circus-loving Henri J. M. Nouwen, the guide of souls who devised a theology of the flying trapeze. "It's very important for me to be as fully present to the moment as I can, but mostly I am out of balance. I am not, though, trying to be a harmonious person but somebody who lives faithfully, works hard, prays deeply, and trusts that God will be there with me."

An antidote to more clinical forms of spirituality, which equate holiness with perfection, Nouwen's life and writings were evidence enough that, even if you feel out of kilter and off balance, you can still be close to God. On the day of our rendezvous, he was on his way, not to a big top as such, but to a large white tent in the heart of the English countryside to speak to young people attending a Christian arts festival. As we greeted each other in a hotel lobby, it was difficult to believe that the tall, bespectacled figure in front of me, with his flat cap, plaid scarf, gray sweater, red bag, and papers, was not on his way to the races. I kept asking myself if this could really be the internationally renowned author of books I had been admiring for years but, at the same time, had no idea who else I

might have been expecting. He was an ordinary looking man with
an extraordinary talent and, as the conversation unfolded, it soon
became apparent that the priest and the broadcaster were much
on each other's wavelengths. I was eager to learn more about the
spiritual artistry of this Dutch master, even if it was for a BBC
radio series. Journalism is a wonderful cover for getting to meet
all your heroes in life, so long as you don't idolize them (at least
during the interview). To reflect the restless nature of Nouwen's
spirit, the program was interspersed with the jazz violin playing
of Stéphane Grappelli, who cofounded the Quintette du Hot Club
de France.

At the time, the sixty-year-old former professor had been living
for a number of years as a pastor to the developmentally disabled
and their assistants at Daybreak, the L'Arche community in Richmond Hill, Ontario. An intense and passionate pastor, Nouwen
needed both security and adventure. At a time when most people
would be calculating their retirement pensions, Nouwen decided to
follow a team of South African trapeze artists for a series of European tours. He said he was struck by the courage of performers
who danced in the air. The fliers lived dangerously until they were
caught by the strong hands of their partners. It was a feat of trust.
As Nouwen observes:

Before they can be caught, they must let go. They must brave
the emptiness of space.

Living with this kind of willingness to let go is one of the
greatest challenges we face. Whether it concerns a person, possession, or personal reputation, in so many areas we hold on
at all costs. We become heroic defenders of our dearly gained
happiness. We treat our sometimes inevitable losses as failures
in the battle of survival.

The great paradox is that it is in letting go, we receive. We
find safety in unexpected places of risk. And those who try
to avoid all risk, those who would try to guarantee that their
hearts will not be broken, end up in a self-created hell.[2]

The physicality of the performers, moreover, raised the curtain on theological possibility for Henri Nouwen. In his eyes, the body told a spiritual story. It was an expression of the spirit of a human person. Real spirituality was about being "enfleshed." There could be no divine life outside the body because, through the Incarnation, God had decided to become body. When you touch a body, in a sense you touch also the divine life. After hours watching the troupe soar through the air, high above a net, Nouwen concluded that their act was a powerful metaphor for the spiritual life. It was about letting go and being caught, an especially reassuring image for those who were dying. For Nouwen, resurrection is not merely a theological construct but a conviction that God catches the person who dies. In *Our Greatest Gift,* he writes:

> Dying is trusting in the catcher. To care for the dying is to say, "Don't be afraid. Remember that you are the beloved child of God. He will be with you when you make your long jump. Don't try to grab him; he will grab you. Just stretch out your arms and hands and trust, trust, trust.[3]

Nouwen researched acrobatic technique with such precision that his voluminous notes seemed destined to resource his most original book to date, but did he not live long enough to shape the text. It is worth pointing out that, wherever I lecture on Nouwen, the spirituality of the flying trapeze triggers most curiosity and questions. But it was just one act in a personal drama hallmarked by highs and lows.

A Mystic of Moods

Born in Nijkerk, Holland, on January 24, 1932, Henri Jozef Machiel Nouwen was the eldest of four. Ordained to the Roman Catholic priesthood in the archdiocese of Utrecht in 1957, he went on to spend seven years as a student of psychology at the Catholic University of Nijmegen. He then enrolled as a fellow in the program for religion and psychiatry at the Menninger Foundation in

Topeka, Kansas, the first national psychiatric hospital of its kind. Its founders believed people with mental illness could be helped and treated at a time when custodial care or permanent social exile were the only alternatives. A high-profile academic career — notably as a professor at Notre Dame, Yale, and Harvard — paralleled Nouwen's emergence as a religious writer who dexterously integrated the worlds of psychology and theology through a semiautobiographical lens of struggle and faithfulness.

A mystic of moods and feelings, Henri Nouwen claimed the heart as the source of our physical, emotional, intellectual, volitional, and moral energies. The way to God was only through the heart. He followed the teachings of the desert fathers, who said that to enter the heart was to enter the kingdom of God. He liked to quote the Russian mystic Theophan the Recluse: "To pray is to descend with the mind into the heart, and there to stand before the face of the Lord, ever-present, all-seeing within you."[4] In *The Way of the Heart*, Nouwen writes:

> From the heart arise unknowable impulses as well as conscious feelings, moods, and wishes. The heart, too, has its reasons and is the center of perception and understanding. Finally, the heart is the seat of the will: it makes plans and comes to good decisions. Thus the heart is the central and unifying organ of our personal life.[5]

No stranger to the paralyzing power of fear, Nouwen was not afraid, though, to share his vulnerability on the page, swiftly gaining respect as a tried and tested "wounded healer" who understood the complex dynamics of the human heart as the intimate core of personal experience and encounter with God. For him, insecurity was not simply an expression of neurosis but a vocation that could lead to a deep spiritual life. The challenge for Nouwen always revolved around the need to become so convinced of God's love for him that human affirmations were not necessary. But it proved to be a lifelong battle. From his psychospiritual trials, however, Nouwen managed to forge an experiential spirituality, rooted in and emerging from a

self-knowledge that the wound of loneliness could become a source
of healing for others, once it was recognized and owned. He sensed
that by tracing his own struggles to their source, he could determine
a level where they might be shared. The spiritual methodology was
not about providing answers or solutions but about encouraging
others that the search for God and ourselves was worth the effort
and pain because, lying at the heart of the arduous journey, were
life-giving signs of hope, courage, and confidence. By accepting the
reality of human anxiety, people could be led into a growing awareness of the different poles between which their lives both vacillated
and were held in tension — between their sense of loneliness and
solitude, their feelings of hostility and hospitality toward others,
and between their illusions about their own immortality and the
true life of prayer.

The Polarities of Spiritual Living

Like Merton, whose influence is always noticeable, Nouwen has an
acute sense of calling and an openness to the process of conversion,
not least through *solitude,* which is not a therapeutic retreat center
in the country but a critical place where the old self can die and
the new self can be born. It is where Christ remodels us in his own
image and liberates us from the compulsions of the world. Solitude
is the way in which we can grow into the realization that where
we are most alone, we are most loved by God. It is a quality of
the heart that helps us accept our aloneness as a divine gift. Then it
becomes possible to convert the aloneness into deep solitude from
where we can reach out to others. In this way, a healthy sense of
community can be realized because people are not clinging to one
another out of loneliness.

A popular companion on the inner journey, Nouwen felt that
writing about the spiritual life was similar to making prints from
negatives. It was not possible to talk about light without darkness,
he told me. The negatives were the dark sides of our lives. But when
we allowed people to see them so they could come in touch with

the light, we were made prints of negatives. To talk about solitude, a positive state, Nouwen first had to speak about loneliness. The life of Jesus Christ was proof enough that the road to salvation (or wholeness) did not have bypasses. The long and painful journey toward human and spiritual integration was all-embracing and all-inclusive. Suffering and joy, intrinsic to any movement toward wholeness, could never be isolated from one another.

"Loneliness is about feeling isolated and separate," he said. "Solitude is about dealing with your aloneness in a positive way. You say: 'I feel alone but [I am] well. I claim my aloneness. I embrace it as a source of life.' To speak about solitude is basically making a print of the negative which is loneliness. It's a way of living and can take a lifetime. Every day I feel lonely again. Every moment that is new, I discover my loneliness at a deep level. I have to keep choosing to convert that loneliness into solitude. The whole spiritual life is a constant choice to let your negative spiritual experiences become an opportunity for conversion and renewal, whether it's despair, doubt, loneliness, sexual confusion, or anger. We have to really look at these, not put them away and live virtuously. It's much more like trusting that, if I embrace my loneliness, depression, and struggle in faith that, somewhere, in the middle, I find light and hope.

"In the world sadness and gladness are always separate. If you are sad, you cannot be glad. If you are glad, you cannot be sad. We say: 'Be happy so we can forget all our troubles.' In the spiritual life it's precisely the opposite. Sadness and gladness can never be separate. You embrace your sadness and trust that, right there, you will find gladness. That is what the cross is all about. You look at the cross, a sign of execution, pain, and torture. But you say: 'Well, the cross is my hope. The cross is a source of life for me. The cross brings me joy.' By embracing the pain, you are speaking about joy. That's a very, very spiritual thing."

Henri Nouwen discovered that, in sharing his faith as a writer and preacher, he was obliged to mention his doubt as well. It was the same with hope and despair or joy and sadness. "If you want to speak about salvation, redemption, or freedom, it is very important they you are willing to speak about what you are being redeemed or set free from," he continued. "I felt I could only speak about it by getting in touch with what I lived. If ministry is to speak about God's redemptive love, I have to witness with my whole being and say: 'I am one who needs to be redeemed and I want to share the struggles that I am living to see how the gospel responds to these struggles.' Jesus says: 'The good shepherd lays down his life for his friends.' If I want to be a good shepherd for people, I have to lay down my life for my friends. I cannot lay half of it down, the nice, sweet, positive things. Moreover, I discovered that the more I shared my anguish, the more people were able to say that they knew what I was talking about. They started taking things a little more seriously when I said there was a way out too." This approach had been a personal catharsis at times, he said. Writing was initially a means to integrate his experiences. He did not consider whether his words would be of value to others. His primary concern had always been to be honest with himself, to know what he was living, to get in touch with his experiences, and to trust that he would eventually discover if they could be useful to people.

Despite authoring more than forty books, Nouwen said he did not have many opportunities to write, although they tended to be connected with intense experiences. When his mother died, for example, writing became an expression of grief. He did not, at first, intend those thoughts to find their way into print but, as people he knew seemed to draw strength from them, he reasoned that a wider audience might also appreciate what he had written.

A Refraction of Love

A vibrant communicator of the Christian faith, Nouwen taught that the spiritual life was one guided by the Spirit of God, the same Spirit that had guided the life of Jesus. Spiritual discipline was the concentrated effort to create space where the Spirit of God could touch, guide, speak, and lead people to unexpected places where they found themselves no longer in control. The core experience of Jesus's public life was his baptism in the Jordan, when he had heard the affirmation: "You are my beloved on whom my favor rests." The entire life of Jesus had been about claiming that identity in the midst of everything. Prayer was about listening to the voice that called each person the beloved. It meant opening your heart in order to enter into communion with the one who loved you before you could love. This "first love" was disclosed to us in prayer. Nouwen believed we should go back time and again to that first love in which we were created, redeemed, and made holy. As an act of returning, prayer was about constantly going back to the truth of our spiritual identity and claiming it for ourselves. That was the meaning of faith. A contemplative discipline required people to divest themselves of all false belongings and identities so that they could become free to belong to God and God alone. Each person was a different refraction of the same love of God, the same light of the world, coming toward us. "*We* can't see God in the world," he would say. "Only God can see God in the world. If I have discovered God as the center of my being, then the God in me recognizes God in the world. Do we see God with our own eye that wants to please or control—or with God's eye?"

A preacher with a message independent of any theological movement, Nouwen believed the future of Western Christianity depended on the ability of people to live mystically. The antithesis of any form of religious fundamentalism, this meant journeying by blind faith, not proselytizing with shallow certainties. The mystical life was one in which people could move away from illusion and, through periods of darkness and doubt, grow into a true relationship with the divine. He said that when Christianity failed to claim the truth that everything was in God, it lost its transforming power and was little more than a series of moral obligations. And in order to thwart demonic manipulation, the spiritual life required people to practice a constant vigilance, deepening and enlivening the presence of God in their hearts. Furthermore, to keep a community strong and vibrant, life needed to be viewed as an ongoing process of confession and forgiveness. A quarter of a century before Barack Obama took office and pledged moral honesty, Nouwen diagnosed a national weakness in the United States:

> One of the great problems with the United States is its refusal to confess its sins. What a great difference it would make, for example, if the President could admit mistakes. The dynamics of social compassion have much to do with both individual and communal forms of confession. It is this that gives us eyes that can see God and the Kingdom in the world.[6]

Spiritual life could never be isolated from political life, he said, but not in the sense of a person intentionally trying to be politically relevant. Many great saints and spiritual visionaries of the past wielded considerable political influence, but not because they were seeking it themselves. Historical figures who managed to have most political effect were often people who had not directly focused on it. St. Benedict, for example, changed the cultural map of Europe, not by aspiring to be a politician, but by trying to be faithful to God and his community. Nevertheless, Benedictine spirituality subsequently generated an all-pervasive effect on European social and political structures, not because the monks had been keen to change political structures but because they were intent on being obedient to God. "If you live spiritual life radically, it affects everything," he went on. "The spiritual life is so essential that it affects economics, politics, and social structures. But you don't live the spiritual life in order to affect politics or in order to make social changes."

Spiritual Ambition and Divine Calling

Our conversation turned to vocation, a theme close to Nouwen's heart. We spoke about finding our true callings and the relationship of the divine will to our own practice of discernment. "God's will is the way God loves us," Nouwen said. "For a long time, I felt that my own desire, which was to study psychology and later become a teacher in psychology, was also my vocation. So that my career and my vocation were not in conflict. As a university professor, I believed I was doing God's will and living according to God's love for me. But at one point it suddenly felt there was a conflict between my career and my vocation, that my career no longer allowed me to continue my vocation. Suddenly I was lost and did not know where to go."

Never one to choose the soft option, Nouwen tested his calling by giving up the security of academia and going to live as a missionary in Latin America. After learning Spanish, he moved to Pamplona Alta, a sprawling barrio on the outskirts of the Peruvian desert city of Lima, where countless children would run up, kissing and hugging him. They even used him as a climbing tree (there were no real arbors in that landscape). Nouwen lived on the roof of a Peruvian slum dwelling, observing poverty at close quarters and learning the virtues of gratitude, joy, and playfulness in the midst of suffering and loss. "I saw babies die because of lack of clean water. It was very painful, but, at the same time, I was amazed how God loves the poor. I went to Latin America with the thought that this might be for the rest of my life. I had a very, very important time there but I also learned that I shouldn't stay there. When I came back, friends felt I should be a voice for Latin America in North America. That was a positive way of thinking about it. A negative way was simply that I found it very hard. I did not feel called there. I did not feel that the church in Latin America or even the people were saying: 'Yeah, Henri, we need you.' It was more about my desire to go there. There was a lot of personal and spiritual ambition. But I very soon found out that I wasn't made for that — or that God didn't call me there and that the people didn't call me there. But it was not something I would have liked to have missed. In fact, I am so grateful I had that experience."

Nouwen's months in Peru prepared him for what eventually emerged as his true vocation — to be a pastor at L'Arche. He said he felt called by that community in a way that he had not by the missionary or academic worlds, even though it was a way of living that seemed incompatible with his gifts and personality. So after a university career among the so-called brightest and best, where he was acclaimed for his teaching and his distinguished record of publications, the absent-minded professor forfeited his post at Harvard to work among people with developmental disabilities who had no inkling of his fame and renown but were soon to find out how human he could be. "Everything seemed not to fit me, but God called me there," he said. "In this case God's will was not totally in line with my specific talents." And, as with the street kids of Lima, Nouwen was about to discover that those who were totally dependent on others could radiate a joy and a peace not found anywhere else.

Affectivity and Trust

During a transitional year as a priest in residence at the first L'Arche community in northern France, Nouwen was supported by the spiritual direction of Père Thomas, who provided him with a much-needed, new context within which to raise questions that had been dominating his emotional life. They concerned his constant need for affection and affirmation. Père Thomas told him that, in a highly psychologized culture, affection had become a major concern. People had started to judge themselves in terms of the affection given or denied. The media had reinforced the idea that human affection (being loved, liked, appreciated, praised, and recognized) was the most desired prize in life. The withholding of these forms of affection could drive people into an abyss of loneliness, depression, and even suicide. Many affective nuances had been analyzed with considerable sophistication through a rich language of the mind that allowed people to express how they felt about themselves and others at different times and in different situations. It was precisely this heightened state of psychological consciousness that sometimes prevented people from reaching the place of the heart where the healing powers were hidden. The heart was the place of trust, the deepest source of the spiritual life — the life of faith, hope, and love. Nouwen writes:

Quite often the suggestion is made that the mystical life, a life in which we enter into a unifying communion with God, is the highest fruit and most precious reward of the moral life. The classical distinction between the purifying way, the illuminating way, and the unifying way as the three progressively higher levels of the spiritual life has strengthened this suggestion. Thus we have come to see the mystical life as the life of the happy few who reach the prayer of total surrender.

The great insight of Père Thomas — an insight in which the best of his theology and the best of his pastoral experience with handicapped people merge — is that the mystical life lies at the beginning of our existence and not just at its end. We are born in intimate communion with the God who created us in love. We belong to God from the moment of our conception. Our heart is that divine gift which allows us to trust not just God but also our parents, our family, ourselves, and our world. Père Thomas is convinced that very small children have a deep, intuitive knowledge of God, a knowledge of the heart that, sadly, is often obscured and even suffocated by the many systems of thought we gradually acquire. Handicapped people, who have such a limited ability to learn, can let their heart speak easily and thus reveal a mystical life that for many intelligent people seems unreachable.[7]

Not for the first time, Nouwen came also to a more fervent understanding of his spiritual journey by meditating on a work of art. On this occasion Rembrandt's masterpiece *The Return of the Prodigal Son* provided the inspiration. The embrace between the father and son — which first caught his attention in a poster reproduction at the French community — prized open his soul. Nouwen had recently undertaken an intensive and relentless lecture tour across the United States, speaking about Nicaragua in the Sandinista era. "I was very tired, frazzled, and felt interiorly very fragmented," he told me. "My whole body and mind were extremely exhausted. I felt very alone and very lonely. But when I suddenly saw this experience of belonging and safety, this embrace of love, I said that this was what I most desired — to be welcomed home so fully and so intimately."

Nouwen later felt compelled to travel to the State Hermitage Museum on the banks of the Neva in St. Petersburg, Russia, to see the larger original, spending not hours but days in front of it. Art, for Nouwen, was always a window into the transcendent. Although familiar with the reproduction (which has become almost a universal emblem of religious communities and retreat centers), Nouwen discovered that, within the original oil painting, many surprises were lying in store: "It suddenly made me aware that not only the younger son was there, being embraced by the father, but also the elder son was standing there in a distant, observing way. I was forced by the painting, not only to look at the younger son, but also look at the elder. I decided to wonder if I wasn't as much the elder son as the younger son. On the one hand, I was the younger son who wanted to come home. But I felt I might also be the elder son who was still angry, jealous, and resentful. It was only later that I suddenly came to the awareness that, once home, I might be called to become the father — and to make my own suffering and my own struggle a way of becoming ready to receive others home."

The canvas became for Nouwen a summary of his life, which prompted the question as to whether there was a danger in projecting one's own needs onto a work of art and hoping it would reflect back what one wanted to see. His response came without hesitation: "I don't think it's a danger but, indeed, a painting *allows* me to project a lot of things. But it also allows me to come in touch with things in myself. I am not suggesting Rembrandt expected anybody to use the painting the way I did. But I have that wonderful freedom to look at a painting and to let the painting become an icon that brings me in touch with my deeper self. I was looking at that painting from the perspective of a human being who lives a lot of pain and joy and has a lot of yearnings. The painting had that enormous power to say something about me and, indeed, I projected into the painting a lot of my own struggles. But I was rewarded for that projection by coming to know myself better. Once I had got in touch with that, I had to speak about it, even though it was very personal."

L'Arche ("the Ark") is a family of 130 communities in 30 countries. At his home in France, its founder, Jean Vanier, told me that, by ministering closely to the disabled as a pastor, Nouwen was able to touch the meaning of his own inner pains. "He discovered the disabled as wounded healers and he discovered himself as a wounded healer," he said. "It was about being healed by the rejected and shedding light on Gospels. The kernel of Nouwen revolved around the questions of brokenness and love. There was an unanswered craving that came out in phenomenal anguish but from his poverty sprang an artistic genius of preaching the Gospel message. He shed light on reality through the Gospels and shed light on the Gospels through experience. His crying out for love was not just for human beings but also for God. It was a yearning for an experience of God. That is part of the mystery that was in him."

According to Jean Vanier, the mystery of Nouwen had been "the incredible mercy of God for a broken humanity." He had brought the mystery of a light shining on the Gospels: it was "something about the poverty of humanity, the intelligence of humanity to talk about that poverty and the grace of Jesus."

After moving to Daybreak, near Toronto, following his year in France, Nouwen was thrust into community living, which required great skill and effort. Gone were the days of the professorial lifestyle with personally controlled projects and the privacy of his own apartment. At his new, more public, home in Richmond Hill, Nouwen was not slow in conceding that "everybody sees everything, knows everything and asks everything." Relationships were sometimes difficult and it was hard to "find a way to love well and to be loved well." After the collapse of a close and dependent friendship, Nouwen plunged into despair, moving out of community and into therapy to battle a devastating depression.

Facing the Demons

Always susceptible to states of deep anxiety, Henri Nouwen had invariably managed to support people in similar situations, among them the writer Jim Forest, a friend of Merton as well. Secretary of the Orthodox Peace Fellowship, Forest edits its quarterly journal, *In Communion*. He grew up in Red Bank, New Jersey, but for more than thirty years has lived in Holland, not far from Amsterdam. He originally went to the Netherlands to head the staff of a peace organization, the International Fellowship of Reconciliation. After his wife left him, Forest sank into depression. Nouwen would often ring from Yale to check on his condition as though he were calling from the neighboring town.

"Nobody else did that," said Forest. "I doubt if Merton had been alive he would have done it either. It was something quite remarkable about Henri — knowing when somebody was suffering greatly and being able to show how much he cared. At a certain point he called and asked why I didn't go over to America and stay with him for a while. I said I would love to but could not afford it. Henri said that would arrange for his travel agent to send the ticket. So I went and we celebrated Easter together. After being with him for some days, he suggested it might be helpful if I went up to stay at the Abbey of the Genesee, and he arranged that. This kind of extraordinary caring for another person was something unusual. I could hardly read. I could just go for walks or bicycle rides or listen to music. I wasn't able to write very much. I was more than half-dead. Reading was too much for me, even Henri's or Merton's books. It was total numbness. One of the best things that happened during that period was going and staying with Henri. It was very inspiring. There was this contagious enthusiasm that you could not be untouched by, no matter how you were feeling."

During his time at Yale, Nouwen was approached by a philosopher who was also suffering from depression. Through a number of conversations with Nouwen, he realized how profound emotional states and frailties could be related to the spiritual. Nouwen observed none of the rules of Freudian analysis. There was no question of therapy. "He would not insist on any particular form of spiritual life but his counseling came entirely from that corner," the philosopher pointed out. "For example, I was once complaining about the Catholic services here. Then Nouwen said to me: 'But you told me that you enjoyed going to the High Mass at Christ Church, the Anglican church. Why don't you go there?' " He was never involved in polemics in the church because he didn't think they were important. Spiritually he was a free man. He was not in any school at all. It grew out of his own development. Everything he did was his own.

"In the books, the first thing that is revealed is his extreme vulnerability, the tensions in his own life that he overcame by being spiritual. He could associate his own vulnerability with that of the audience. That was what made him such a gripping person. At the same time, there was no doubt in his mind that the problems in his life and lives of his audience were part of the spiritual texture of life. For him, the spiritual had no halo around it. He was able to speak with modern people in the world with modern problems such as anxiety and disruption. This was his real power and why people read him."

Another person guided through depression by Nouwen happened to be one of his readers. The late Wendy Wilson Greer (who went on to found the Henri Nouwen Society in the United States and Canada) first heard him preach at St. John's, Lafayette Square, Washington, DC, opposite the White House. She said his sermon was so powerful that she began to seek out his books. It was only after a two-year depression, many years later, that she decided to send Nouwen a fourteen-page letter. The author replied sympathetically, enclosing a copy of *The Return of the Prodigal Son,* a popular book about his experiences in front of the Rembrandt painting. "In my letter I had talked about the depression, how his books had helped me and how, no matter what I read of his, I connected with something very deep in him," Wendy Greer told me in her Manhattan apartment overlooking Central Park while I was researching my biography of Nouwen, *Wounded Prophet*.[8] "I didn't really understand that it was probably his own depression that I was connecting with. I don't think I have ever had that with any other writer." In *Heart Speaks to Heart* Nouwen had written about the time he had left Daybreak. He had not used the word "depression," but Wendy Greer intuited that he would understand what she had been through. The following year she managed to meet Nouwen when he was speaking at a conference in North Carolina. He remembered their correspondence and a friendship evolved. Nouwen would often stay in New York with Wendy and her husband, Jay. "When I was working through the depression, I really felt abandoned by God," Wendy explained. "But I did not realize God was there all along. It was a devastating depression and knocked me totally off my feet. But I was able to share my depression with Henri and he talked about his depression. He had the ability to zero into the depths of your soul right away. That was his gift, making friends out of strangers. He just connected with you. He shared not only his pain but your pain."

Anguish and Glory

Wendy Greer eventually persuaded Nouwen to publish a secret journal he had kept during his depression. Living through "an agony that seemed never to end," he had been supported by two guides "as parents hold a wounded child." To his surprise, however, he did not lose the ability to write, and most days, after meeting his guides, he would jot down a "spiritual imperative," a command to himself that had emerged from the session with the therapists. Each was directed to his own heart and not intended to be read by anyone else. Eight years later, the mandates seemed less private and possibly of value to others. They were turned into a book called *The Inner Voice of Love*.[9] Tracing a journey "through anguish to freedom," the meditations show that, at his worst, Nouwen was at his best. In a reflection entitled "Separate the False Pains from the Real Pain," Nouwen writes about rejection:

There is a real pain in your heart, a pain that truly belongs to you. You know now that you cannot avoid, ignore, or repress it. It is this pain that reveals to you how you are called to live in solidarity with the broken human race. You must distinguish carefully, however, between your pain and the pains that have attached themselves to it but are not truly yours. When you feel rejected, when you think of yourself as a failure and a misfit, you must be careful not to let these feelings and thoughts pierce your heart. You are not a failure or a misfit. Therefore, you have to disown these pains as false. They can paralyze you and prevent you from loving the way you are called to love.

It is a struggle to keep distinguishing the real pain from the false pains. But as you are faithful to that struggle, you will see more and more clearly your unique call to love. As you see that call, you will be more and more able to claim your real pain as your unique way to glory.[10]

I remember Nouwen telling me himself how the months of his therapy had been "a hugely painful and an immensely healing time" as he slowly realized that his conflicting struggles and feelings of rejection were transformative in the sense that they enabled him to be a more compassionate priest after his return to L'Arche. He spoke, too, of how the community had taught him the meaning of gratitude — "receiving the gifts of others and discovering them as real gifts for you." The core members and assistants allowed their pastor to see life as gift, especially when it was fragile. It was a process of moving from resentment to gratitude. Nouwen likened resentment to a cold anger in which people felt they had not been given what they believed they needed. It was necessary to let go of that feeling in order to discover there were many gifts for everyone, if only people had the eyes to detect them. Community living enlarged one's heart for that capacity, he said.

L'Arche was also a place where Nouwen discovered more and more of his own disabilities. The directness of the core members put him in touch with stark realities: "Once I came home and brought gifts for everybody in the house. One guy said: 'I don't care for your gifts. Stay home with your gifts. I don't need more gifts. You cover me with too many gifts. I don't even have a place on my wall.' I was very, very hurt. But suddenly I realized he was just touching me in the right place, in a very painful place, that I had used the gifts to replace an intimacy with him that he really wanted. He wanted friendship and here I was giving him gifts. I was not really interested in becoming friends because I didn't really like him terribly much. So I gave him gifts instead, which helped me stay away from intimacy. So he opened up that place and I realized my handicap: that I wasn't always willing to enter into relationships with people who asked me for them." Nouwen's ministry at L'Arche was sealed by faithfulness, energy, and commitment, but he could not be contained by the community, even though it was nourishing him at different levels. He was a creative, restless, driven personality who needed a travel agent as much as a spiritual director. As one of his friends put it wryly: "L'Arche was the center of his absence."

Nouwen's own sudden death, from a heart attack on September 21, 1996, came during one of those absences. He was passing through his native Holland, en route from Toronto to St. Petersburg, to make a film of his book *The Return of the Prodigal Son*.

The tributes poured in, honoring an internationally renowned scholar and wounded healer whose knowledge of what he needed guided him to God — and others in the process. Vulnerability was the signpost. For him, the language of the heart was universal. Through faith, he trusted that his experience would touch another's and, perhaps, bring that person closer to divine encounter.

Fall and Recovery

The influence of Nouwen around the world has not abated. As a retired Anglican priest in South Africa, Father Harry Wiggett has an ongoing pastoral ministry beyond the bounds of the institutional church, working among alcoholics and drug addicts at three recovery centers in Cape Town. Repeatedly he hears that, in the light of their addiction, they have come to regard themselves as society's failures. Bearing a burden of shame, guilt, and a sense of unworthiness, they do not think they would be readily accepted by any faith community. In addition, many have felt either rejected by God, or have rejected any thought of there being a God who could possibly be interested in them, let alone love them. In their search for spirituality and recovery, Father Wiggett has introduced his "Wednesday Friends" to the theology of Henri Nouwen, especially his maxim "Trust the Catcher."

"It is such a joy to tell of the liberating effect that image of the catcher has on folk searching for some meaningful understanding of God," said Harry Wiggett. "One can almost feel a corporate glow of relief as they begin to realize that the only reasonable explanation for each one being in the recovery center and program is that, when they were falling, falling to their very lowest point of hopelessness and helplessness, someone caught them. And so, with no need to elaborate, this dynamic image makes its impression on these searching minds and the seed sown becomes the beginning of a meaningful understanding of God who cares and loves, to whom each person matters and belongs. From that sense of individual belonging comes a deep realization of corporate belonging, of community, of belonging together, to one another — all of which undergirds the spiritual impetus for ongoing progressive healing and wholeness."

Father Henri Nouwen was a brilliant teacher and priest who filtered spiritual concepts through his heart. Between the subjective and the objective lay the personal and interpersonal. As Sister Annice Callahan, RSCJ, adjunct assistant professor of systematic theology at the University of San Diego, told me: "He had the capacity to let his own heart be touched and to touch hearts. I think that was his real gift. He was very drawn to active receptivity and allowed his own heart to be an open book that any of us could read. Although spirituality was becoming an academic discipline in its own right, it could appear academic, esoteric, and erudite. I think

Nouwen was well aware of the hazard. He realized in his own life, perhaps, the wreckage that that had caused in terms of a certain dissociation between his mind and his heart. But because his own heart was so in touch with a variety of disciplines, such as psychology and scripture, there was always a blend. And yet, reading Nouwen's work, I got the impression that he was never in his head, but always in his heart — and that he wanted readers to be in their hearts too. That is the fruit of his work."

Professor Callahan said she would rank Henri Nouwen in the order of Thomas Merton and Dorothy Day, people of spiritual inspiration who had the ability to let their own lives be transformed in a North American context and then, in turn, encouraged others to that same transformation. Nouwen had been countercultural at a time when North America was becoming a consumer-technological society. In his own journey he had recognized the hazards of individualism. "The loneliness of academia had allowed certain aspects of his heart to atrophy and he knew that the connection with the poor and developmentally disabled would just break him open — which it did.

"He was always interested in what was going on in your heart, whether you wanted him to be or not," she said. "He was a soul-barer who believed in following your heart. The habits of heart that remind me of Nouwen are gratitude, trust, and compassion. He repeated these often in his life in different ways but he found they were like the gospel values, the platform of everything he wrote."

A timeless theologian, Nouwen earned his place in the great mystical tradition of Christianity. At a time when spiritual writing in North America had come to mean, at one end of the spectrum, paperbacks about psychological self-improvement and, at the other, rigid tomes of piety, Nouwen was producing year by year popular books of ascetical spirituality influenced by his European education and training. They gained appeal through their clear philosophical, theological, and cultural analysis. Professor George Schner, whom I met at Regis College, Toronto, during my biographical research,

said he believed Nouwen was attempting something that would survive in the long run in the established tradition of ascetical theology.
He had reinvented the Christian spiritual tradition in an innovative
style germane to the times.

Nouwen had continued the Catholic tradition of being intellectually aware and spiritually sensitive. While not pandering to the
currents of the day, he taught a rendition of mainstream Catholicism
using a pertinent, culturally critical, and appropriate methodology.
Western modern contemporary culture had closed off an established
easy access to the transcendent in the world. Psychology, sociology,
philosophy, and theology all had their place, but if the heart, the
inner person, the deepest part of the self, was not open to God,
what was the use of these disciplines? Nouwen had not sold out
deep Christian principles and history to another science or discipline for novelty's sake, said Professor Schner. To some extent
he said the tried and true. But he attempted to give it a correct
rhetoric, assessing the needs of the audience and rediscovering,
in a closed environment, an opening to the transcendent. But the
price Nouwen paid for his own transparency was considerable. His
influence as a spiritual master came at a cost, something he recognized during his depression as he wrote that series of imperatives to
himself:

> You must decide for yourself to whom and when you give
> access to your interior life. For years you have permitted others
> to walk in and out of your life according to *their* needs and
> desires. Thus you were no longer master in your own house,
> and you felt increasingly used. So, too, you quickly became
> tired, irritated, angry, and resentful.
>
> Think of a medieval castle surrounded by a moat. The
> drawbridge is the only access to the interior of the castle. The
> lord of the castle must have the power to decide when to draw
> the bridge and when to let it down. Without such power, he
> can become the victim of enemies, strangers, and wanderers.
> He will never feel at peace in his own castle.

It is important for you to control your own drawbridge. There must be times when you keep your bridge drawn and have the opportunity to be alone or only with those to whom you feel close. Never allow yourself to become public property where anyone can walk in and out at will. You might think that you are being generous in giving access to anyone who wants to enter or leave, but you will soon find yourself losing your soul.

When you claim for yourself the power over your drawbridge, you will discover new joy and peace in your heart and find yourself able to share that joy and peace with others.[11]

But it is debatable whether Nouwen found the joy and peace he so desired. While his extreme vulnerability only increased his credibility as an authentic spiritual thinker, the insecurities that had beset him from childhood haunted him to the end. During his final year, Nouwen began weighing up his responsibilities as a faithful priest and as a beloved writer with opportunities for more permanent forms of intimacy and new expressions of ministry. Like many priests, he wrestled daily with the requirements of celibacy and the living out of his sexual orientation. Feelings of loneliness and abandonment were never far from the surface. But unlike the trapeze artist, he could not let go and completely embrace another form of life, even though part of him longed to. He recognized within the beauty of that circus act a joy and freedom to which he aspired — and which he deserved. There were new possibilities on the horizon, and it is sad they were denied him. As Nouwen himself writes:

After ten years of living with people with mental disabilities and their assistants, I have become deeply aware of my own sorrow-filled heart. There was a time when I said: "Next year I will finally have it together," or "When I grow more mature these moments of inner darkness will go," or "Age will diminish my emotional needs." But now I know that my sorrows are mine and will not leave me. In fact I know they are very old

and very deep sorrows, and that no amount of positive thinking or optimism will make them less. The adolescent struggle
to find someone to love me is still there; unfulfilled needs for
affirmation as a young adult remain alive in me. The deaths of
my mother and many family members and friends during my
later years cause me continual grief. Beyond all that, I experience deep sorrow that I have not become who I wanted to
be, and that the God to whom I have prayed so much has not
given me what I have most desired.[12]

These are poignant words, which suggest that Nouwen may not
have been as settled at L'Arche as some of his other writings implied.
Always faithful to his sense of calling, he continued to struggle
with his needs for personal intimacy. Many priests strongly identified with him. Contemporaries in a similar predicament either went
completely into the institution as an escape or moved completely
out of it and identified with another culture. Nouwen pitched his
tent in the gap and found meaning in the flying trapeze.

It is all too easy to want to sanitize our spiritual masters, cloaking
them in the clichés of hagiography. When they die, it is inevitable
that different groups and individuals will try to claim them as their
own. Such reverence can, of course, take the form of near celebrity
obsession as devotees try to clasp their memory in death. There is
nothing unhealthy about having spiritual heroes — we need them
more than ever in a consumerist culture — but worshiping them is
clearly perilous. This is one reason why researching an honest book
about a spiritual figure can be tantamount to crossing a minefield
at night. The battlefield of biography is never more dangerous than
when the subject is a spiritual guide, and it is almost impossible
to avoid the crossfire. "Don't shoot the messenger" can echo as
much across the chambers of theological portraiture as it can in the
domain of secular news journalism.

The reality is that, no matter how influential our spiritual guides
become and how much we want to idolize them, they are not always
in balance. Many wrestle with ambiguities and uncertainties until

their last breath. Angst was the signature tune of Nouwen, who brought hope and faith to millions through the struggles he dared to share.

We are not the healers, we are not the reconcilers, we are not the givers of life. We are sinful, broken, vulnerable people who need as much care as anyone we care for. The mystery of ministry is that we have been chosen to make our own limited and very conditional love the gateway for the unlimited and unconditional love of God.[13]

FOUR

The Monk and the Professor

Conversations about Merton and Nouwen

Although Henri Nouwen and Thomas Merton are often twinned as a spiritual fraternity, they were, in fact, different personalities writing for diverse audiences, which is not to deny resonances between them. Nouwen was undoubtedly influenced by Merton's keeping of journals. On May 7, 1967, at the height of Merton's fame, Nouwen went to the Abbey of Gethsemani to meet his spiritual hero. Both recorded the encounter. Merton did not, however, recollect Nouwen's name, referring to him in his journal as "Father Nau." The entry in *Learning to Love* was subsequently amended:

Yesterday the new Archbishop McDonough was here — I did not go to hear him speak. Ran into Raymond's friend Alexis — the South African from Notre Dame — and Fr. [Henri] Nouwen (Dutch psychologist teaching at N[otre] D[ame], had a good talk in the evening by the lake in Charlie O'Brien's pasture (old name for St. Bernard's field).[1]

Nouwen's recollection of the meeting is more personally felt and significant:

I met him only once, at the Abbey of Our Lady of Gethsemani in Kentucky. Yet thereafter, his person and work had such an impact on me, that his sudden death stirred me as if it were the death of one of my closest friends. It therefore seems natural for me to write for others about the man who has inspired me most in recent years.[2]

91

Thomas Merton: Contemplative Critic, first published by
Nouwen in 1976, is written as an introduction to Merton's life
and thought. It includes a commentary ("For Instruction") on
contemplation, silence, solitude, social justice, and the wisdom of
the East. The second section ("For Meditation") complements the
first with themed quotations from the writings. It is evident that
Nouwen is steeped in the spirituality of the man, the passion and
the paradoxes, the prophecy and the prayer.

As Henri Nouwen's own career as an author gathered momen-
tum in the immediate years after Merton's death, he came to be
known as the "authentic successor" to the monk in the realm of
spiritual writing. Some people who bought Merton's books were
also drawn the writings of Nouwen, even if it became evident in
the reading of them that the Dutchman was a more emotional figure who was not reticent in making his private hurts public. Merton
remained a person of inspiration for Nouwen throughout his teaching career and, in his own way, Nouwen may well have tried to
emulate him. It was not surprising, therefore, that Nouwen quit
academia for a while in the 1970s to test his vocation with the Trappists. *The Genesee Diary,* written during that sabbatical, proved to
be one of Nouwen's most engaging books.[3] Dedicated "to all contemplative men and women who by their commitment to unceasing
prayer offer us hope in the midst of a troubled world," it is a candid
chronicle of the cloisters. Merton is clearly in Nouwen's thoughts
as he relives his day:

> One of the things that strikes me is that Merton is like the
> Bible: he can be used for almost any purpose. The conser-
> vative and the progressive, the liberal and the radical, those
> who fight for changes and those who complain about them,
> political activists and apolitical utopians, they all quote Mer-
> ton to express their ideas and convictions. . . . Merton never
> tried to be systematic and never worried about being consis-
> tent. He articulated skillfully and artfully the different stages
> of his own thoughts and experiences and moved on to new

discoveries without worrying about what people made of his old ones. Now he is dead. He can no longer answer the question, "What did you really man?" He probably would only have been irritated by such a question. But his death has made him an even stronger catalyst than he was during his life. He indeed made his own life available to others to help them find their own — and not his — way. In this sense, he was and still is a true minister, creating the free space where others can enter and discover God's voice in their lives.[4]

"A Poet and a Popularizer"

"There was no doubt that Thomas Merton's writings meant a great deal to Henri Nouwen. But anybody who thinks that Nouwen was the Merton of his generation either did not know Henri or did not know Merton." The words are of Father John Eudes Bamberger, who entered the Abbey of Gethsemani in 1950 and was a scholastic under Merton from 1952 until 1955. A medical doctor before becoming a monk, he later trained as a psychiatrist. John Eudes and Merton lived in the same community for eighteen years. Merton was his spiritual director and they worked closely together receiving and assessing postulants. Nouwen was counseled by Father John Eudes at Gethsemani during a time of crisis in his life, and they kept in touch over the years. In 1971, three years after Merton's death, John Eudes was elected abbot of Our Lady of the Genesee in Piffard, upstate New York.

"Thomas Merton and Henri Nouwen were very different types of people," Father John Eudes told me. "They wrote to a different audience and wrote to different levels of experience. Merton was really a born artist and literary figure. Henri was basically a teacher and a communicator on the popular level, whereas, in my opinion, Merton really wrote for a more specialized group in terms of his personal experience. The opinions people had of his writings did not influence Merton very much unless they were artists. He was very serious about the peace movement and social justice, but when it came to his role as a writer, I think he wrote for a very specialized group and a very different group than Henri wrote for.

"Merton was basically a poet, while Henri wasn't. He was more clear and a popularizer. I think that is a high calling. I think that a priest is called to do that sort of thing. But I believe Merton was a very unusual type of person, and I don't think Henri was. Henri was very intelligent and devoted, but he wasn't gifted at all in the same way that Merton was. Merton had a terrific amount of energy and an unusual kind of intelligence. Henri was very energetic, very devoted, and reasonably intelligent, but he wasn't extraordinarily intelligent. Merton was.

"I don't think you could find any original ideas in Henri's work, but that was his mission and he understood that. Henri was such a sympathetic person that he tended — and Merton in a different way had some of that same quality — to throw himself into things so much that he identified with his audience more than Merton did. Merton identified with a certain level of his audience and then, if you didn't get it, that was your problem. It didn't worry him too much. But I think Henri would have been uncomfortable about that, although person-to-person Merton was also very inclined to go as far as he could to agree with people, which is why many, I think, were misled by him, because it didn't change his mind at all. I think that was the chief difference between the two.

"Henri was identifying deeply with his own spiritual values and finding his way into prayer. He was bringing together his emotional life and his life of prayer and then relating them to daily experience, which is the monastic approach. Prayer for a monk is a way of life. It's not just one activity among many, or even the most important activity. It is something that permeates the whole of one's existence, and I think Henri was trying to approach that. In seven months nobody achieves that, and he was smart enough to know it. I think, during one phase, he thought he might do better to think of becoming a monk, but that was just a normal, understandable reaction. I don't think it was ever a serious issue for him. Merton, however, was a very deeply committed monk and, although other people tried to get him to leave the monastery, he himself said that he never really took that seriously, except for five minutes once. With Henri it was quite the opposite, and for very good reasons. He felt that his time here worked, that it helped him very much to point out the ways he could approach his spiritual life while still remaining active."

Father John Eudes said he thought at the time that *The Genesee Diary* would be helpful to others in a way that Merton's work was not. Nouwen's difficulties had been the kind most people faced when they spent time in a monastic context. Nouwen had peace up to a point, but, as the diary showed, he encountered a range of emotional issues that were not uncommon. Merton had them too but did not commit them to print. He wrote from the perspective of a person who had assimilated and reinterpreted those issues. High literary prose became the vehicle for expressing what he had experienced. "But he did it with such naturalness that an unsophisticated reader would be led to think that that was the way it worked. But it didn't. It's like reading the prophet Isaiah, who was a great poet and a deeply religious, contemplative person. There aren't many people who are capable of that kind of experience — but many people can learn from it. You can take what you're up to, but you won't function the way he did. That's the difference between the two people. What Henri experienced was a kind of large version of what the average intelligent, devoted, and serious person will run into."

Points of Divergence

As I mentioned in the previous chapter, Jim Forest (who authored an elegant, pictorial biography of the monk, *Living with Wisdom*)[5] was a friend of both. Forest's contact with Merton had begun through correspondence in the summer of 1961, not long after he had been discharged from the U.S. Navy. He had recently joined the Catholic Worker community in New York City, a house of hospitality mainly for street people in a part of Manhattan now known as the East Village. His first letter to Merton led to many more. For more than seven years, until Merton's death, Forest wrote to Merton on average once a month. There were letters, cards, and copies of manuscripts from Merton at about the same rate. Sometimes packages arrived — an occasional box of monastery-made cheese with a gift card signed "Uncle Louie." There were also two extended visits with Merton at the monastery, one early in 1962, another late in 1964.

At his home in Alkmaar, a city in the Dutch province of North Holland, Jim Forest recalled the day Henri Nouwen invited him to talk to theology students at Yale about Thomas Merton. At the time Forest was a member of the Emmaus community in East Harlem, New York, which had a vision similar to that of the Catholic Worker. Merton had been dead for only a few years and Forest had started writing about him. "Merton and I were very close," Jim Forest told me. "I was able to tell the students stories about Merton and describe what he was like as a person. In the process I got to know Henri, and I spoke to the students about him every year until Henri left Yale. It's hard to compare the two of them. But the points they had in common were also quite striking — two people who remained in the priesthood at a time when a great many were leaving ministry in the church. Neither of them did so. Priesthood was so much part of who they were."

Forest said that the primary impact on Merton's life had come from the phenomenal response to his autobiography, *The Seven Storey Mountain*. Out of that had emerged a community of readers who turned out to be extremely loyal. Anyone who read that book would be drawn into his other writing. Nouwen failed to write an equivalent book. That was the difference. Another divergence was that Nouwen was not attracted to the Asian spiritual traditions. He was more intrigued by healing — his own and everybody else's. Merton was not particularly bothered by that. One of the surprising traits of Merton was a remarkable range of interests, from the novels of Faulkner to tiny religious cults in the Pacific islands. It would be possible to make books of Merton's writings hardly knowing he was a Trappist monk, even though his sensibility was clearly informed by that way of living. He was often absent in his writings and, on the whole, did not betray his emotional responses to events or people. He sometimes wrote about his enthusiasms with a certain detachment, relatively speaking, that Nouwen never even attempted. Nouwen was never detached from anything he wrote about and did not pretend to be, even to the point of occasionally embarrassing his readers. "It was hard to think what Merton was not interested in, but you could make a long list of things that did not particularly interest Nouwen," said Forest. "One of those was Buddhism. But the few things he was interested in absolutely interested him, and that fascination would continue for years."

Spiritual Fathers

Evident in both authors was an attraction to the undivided church, the church at the roots of predenominational Christianity (alluded to earlier by Archbishop Rowan Williams). It was not a cheap ecumenism. Both were looking for matters of deep importance here and now, and both had contributed to some extent to the restoration of the church in their lifetime. At a certain point Nouwen had realized that people were more responsive to stories when they were related intimately than when they were told in a more abstract manner. If he talked about how he came to realize something through the struggle of his own life, not everyone might feel comfortable. But for many readers in the United States, this was precisely what made his spiritual insights accessible. "He was a man through whom you could experience God's mercy. That's not something you can say about so many people," said Forest. "By talking about some of his own struggles, Henri made it easier for you to talk about yours." At different periods, Thomas Merton and Henri Nouwen were spiritual fathers to Jim Forest. Both were excellent confessors, he said. They made it possible for him to share parts of himself that were painful, awkward, or embarrassing. Each helped him survive hard times and cope with periods of despair.

As spiritual guides for their respective generations and beyond, they were harnessed by restlessness. Both were Europeans who had made their home in North America. As Catholic priests, both lived a life that was centered in the liturgy. Both were deeply sensitive to the suffering of others. They were involved in opposition to war and social injustice, for which they were sometimes regarded as liberals or even radicals, yet both were passionately devoted to promoting the spiritual life and took a dim view of popular political ideologies, for which they were sometimes regarded as conservatives.

"After he wrote his autobiography, which seemed to say there was no better place on earth to be than the Abbey of Our Lady of Gethsemani in rural Kentucky, many of Merton's letters in later years almost catch fire with complaints about the shortcomings of life in his chosen monastery," Forest pointed out. "On several occasions Merton sought permission to leave with the idea of sharing in the life of a poorer, smaller, more primitive monastery either in Latin America or some other part of the world. One of the amazing achievements of his life was that he not only was steadfast in his monastic vocation but remained a monk of the Abbey of Gethsemani until his death. Still there was a basic restlessness. It is somehow appropriate that he died on pilgrimage on the other side of the planet while attending a monastic conference in Thailand after weeks of travel in India and Sri Lanka.

"Henri had no monastic vows to limit his travel, nor was his bishop in Utrecht inclined to rein him in. His restlessness brought him from Holland to America. He taught at Notre Dame, then Yale, then Harvard, but could bring himself to stay at none of these distinguished institutions. Searching for community, he was a kind of temporary brother at a Trappist monastery for several extended periods, but found that, while monastic life helped clear his mind, it didn't ultimately suit him. He had a sabbatical in Latin America and thought for a time he was called to make his life there as a missionary, but then decided that also wasn't his calling. He finally found a home for himself not in academia or monastic life but with the L'Arche community in Canada — not the brilliant but the people with developmental disabilities plus their downwardly mobile assistants. Even then he was often on the move."

Icons of the Church

Merton and Nouwen shared a passionate interest in the desert fathers and both published collections of desert father stories. They were drawn to hesychasm, a "resting prayer" originally fostered by desert monasticism in Egypt and Palestine. Both had a deeply established practice of the Jesus Prayer, which lies at the core of the hesychastic spiritual tradition. ("Lord Jesus Christ, have mercy on me a sinner.") Both appreciated icons and wrote about them. Both were attentive to Orthodox teachers of prayer. Jim Forest recognized in Nouwen a visual sensitivity and the rare gift of being able to reveal in a nonacademic way various aspects of a painting to another person. There was a certain discipline in it but one always had the sense of absolute freedom in his way of describing it.

Merton, son of artists, had an artistic gift in his own right, and his own artwork has found its way into print. As a young man, he had visited some of Rome's most ancient churches — San Clemente, Santa Sabina, Santa Maria Maggiore, Cosmas and Damian, the Lateran, Santa Costanza, Santa Maria in Trastevere, and San Prassede. These moved him in an unexpected and extraordinary way. Forest told me that on the walls of the more ancient churches in Rome, Merton had found Byzantine mosaics not unlike the icon drawings his father had been making shortly before his death. Merton's first encounter with ancient Christian art came as he stood in front of a fresco in a ruined chapel. Although he did not realize it at the time, Byzantine mosaics were to play their part in his unfolding spiritual pilgrimage. Through these icons, Merton said that he began to understand, not simply who Christ was, but who Christ is. He experienced a profound sense of peace beside them and a strong conviction that he belonged there.

Nouwen published a book on icons, *Behold the Beauty of the Lord*,[6] that Merton would have loved, said Forest, himself a member of the Orthodox Church. It remains among the best introductions to icons. He recalled how Nouwen had once visited him in Holland and brought with him a reproduction of Rublev's Holy Trinity icon that he had purchased that morning in a shop in Paris. Though Forest had not yet seen the actual icon — it was in the Tretyakov Gallery in Moscow — Henri had been confident that the print came as close to the real thing as print technology would allow.

For Nouwen and Merton, the icon was the primary visual art of the church — if not the door, then the window. It had to be appreciated as something meaningful as part of the totality of the church. Icons became dead plants when seen simply as works of art, aesthetic objects, or collectors' items. They were intimately connected with the Eucharistic life and daily prayer of the spiritual community. Both writers, concluded Jim Forest, had played a major role in the quiet movement of rediscovering icons.

"Both had a remarkable gift for communicating to others the fact that a life of faith is one of endless exploration, an adventure second to none," he said.

What writers like Nouwen and Merton illustrate is that, whatever people might think about this being a secular age, it is possible for highly contemporary people, with all the cultural ticks, mannerisms, and instinctive reactions of the age, to live in the world of Christian practice and sacramental faith — and find it life-giving. That was important in itself, said the Archbishop of Canterbury, Dr. Rowan Williams, as we reflected on the two spiritual authors during our conversation at Lambeth Palace. But Dr. Williams felt there was a more profound value to their writings. "All of us," he continued, "who are trying to lead honest and fruitful lives that are open to the truth of God need to have stories of those who do it and those who make the journey — and I won't say survive because, of course, they don't — but are changed in that crucible."

The archbishop added: "I would have liked to hear Anthony de Mello talking to Henri Nouwen or Thomas Merton because de

Mello is very ruthless about pictures of yourself. I think he would have given both Merton and Nouwen quite a hard time about their constant picturing and framing of themselves. De Mello is very, very hard in that sense, and yet what saves Merton and Nouwen, is that they go on questioning the pictures of themselves that they generate. That is a good model for us."

FIVE

Deconditioning the Mind

The Awakening of Anthony de Mello

The disciples were full of questions about God.

Said the master: "God is the Unknown and the Unknowable. Every statement about him, every answer to your questions, is a distortion of the truth."

The disciples were bewildered. "Then why do you speak about him at all?"

"Why does the bird sing?" said the master.

"Not because it has a statement, but because it has a song," comments Anthony de Mello. "The words of the scholar are to be understood. The words of the master are not to be understood. They are to be listened to as one listens to the wind in the trees and the sound of the river and the song of the bird. They will awaken something within the heart that is beyond all knowledge."[1]

An Indian retreat leader and spiritual director who did not believe in the need to find ultimate answers, de Mello gained international popularity after the stories, parables, and meditations that exemplified his teaching were turned into books that sold in their millions, not least in Latin America. A Jesuit priest who skillfully integrated Western and Eastern spiritual traditions, he tried to show in wise, humorous (and sometimes mischievous), ways that the psychological walls that imprison people were simply mental constructs with no basis in reality. For him, the unaware life was not worth living, and his mission was to open it up.

As well as quoting from the Old and New Testaments, including the sayings of Jesus, de Mello borrowed freely from Hasidic, Sufi, and Zen masters. However, because he drew increasingly (and sometimes exclusively) from Hindu and Buddhist sources — and was sometimes circumspect about his own beliefs — some people questioned his allegiance to the Christian faith. After his death, the Vatican investigated his writings.

But de Mello never really strayed from his aim of trying to awaken his listeners and readers to an awareness of God's presence in their lives, as Christ himself had done. Christ had not been an earnest imparter of ecclesiastical doctrines but, like de Mello, was a consummate storyteller who wanted to awaken his listeners to new life and the offer of salvation. Christ, he said, had startled people out of their preconceived notions of religion with a message that had been so shattering it had led him to the cross. Following Christ meant not external conformation but interior conversion:

> You know, sometimes people want to imitate Christ but, when a monkey plays a saxophone, that doesn't make him a musician. You can't imitate Christ by imitating his external behavior. You've got to be Christ. Then you'll know exactly what to do in a particular situation, given your temperament, your character, and the character and temperament of the person you're dealing with. No one has to tell you. But to do that, you must be what Christ was. An external imitation will get you nowhere.[2]

But for anyone undertaking the inner journey, God is beyond words, concepts, or doctrinal formulas. It is simply not possible to know God. The moment you give a flower a name, you lose the reality. As soon as you give God a name, you lose God. De Mello once told a friend: "What and who and how God, Ultimate Reality, is, I do not know: I make an act of trust and occasionally I experience Him as merciful."[3]

An Alarm Clock for a Sleeping World

In his writings, Anthony de Mello is not afraid to shock — or even to hurt — so long as he stabs people awake. People live in a state of hypnosis, he maintains, and are not aware that their minds have been conditioned to think and behave in certain ways. In relationships, for example, people depend on each other emotionally and issue demands to protect their happiness. This need to control arises from a fear of loss, alienation, and rejection. But loneliness cannot be cured by human company, says the spiritual master, but by contact with reality:

> Where there is love, there are no demands, no expectations, no dependency. I do not demand that you make me happy; my happiness does not lie in you. If you were to leave me, I will not feel sorry for myself; I enjoy your company immensely, but I do not cling. I enjoy it on a non-clinging basis. What I really enjoy is not you; it's something that's greater than both you and me. It's something that I discovered, a kind of symphony, a kind of orchestra that plays one melody in your presence but, when you depart, the orchestra doesn't stop. When I meet someone else, it plays another melody, which is also very delightful. And when I'm alone, it continues to play. There's a great repertoire and it never ceases to play. That's what awakening is all about.[4]

Enlightenment, then, is about seeing people as they are — not as we would wish them to be. When we are let down or hurt by others, the blame lies at our own door for expecting too much of them in the first place. We paint them in glowing colors, instead of seeing them as human beings who, like us, are asleep, with their own self-interests at heart:

> Can you imagine how liberating it is that you'll never be disillusioned again, never be disappointed again? You'll never feel let down again. Never feel rejected. Want to wake up? You want happiness? You want freedom? Here it is: Drop

your false ideas. See through people. If you see through yourself, you will see through everyone. Then you will love them. Otherwise you spend the whole time grappling with your wrong notions of them, with your illusions which are constantly crashing against reality.[5]

De Mello, then, is an alarm clock for a somnolent world. For him, spirituality is about rising from the slumbers and getting in touch with reality. As a spiritual guide, he intrigues and fascinates but is hard to pin down and categorize. Like the message itself, his teaching eludes neat packaging (and deliberately so). De Mello's books are not theological tomes but compendiums of wisdom to be taken in small doses, in much the same way as we might consult a medical almanac. The source of many psychological and spiritual problems, argues de Mello, can be traced to the way churches have tried to control their congregations. People become burdened by the negative emotions of dissatisfaction, guilt, and inadequacy because the moralistic side of religion goads them to change and perform. This is not only unhealthy but constitutes a form of inner brutality that has the potential to breed outer expressions of violence. Spiritual growth is not about being weighted down with negativity but about dying to oneself and casting off religion's tyrannical hold.

Imagination and Reality

De Mello proposes a four-step guide to wisdom, which involves first getting in touch with negative feelings (such as self-hatred or guilt) we might not even be aware of. We have, then, to grasp the fact that the feeling is in us and not in reality. The third step is to stop identifying with the feeling that has nothing to do with the "I." We should not define our intrinsic selves with any such feeling. We should say, "I am experiencing depression," rather than "I am depressed." The final step lies in recognizing the need for change in ourselves rather than in others. We always want someone else to change, says de Mello, so that we will feel good. But we ourselves need the medicine. The mystics did not say, "I feel good because the world is right," but "The world is right because I feel good."

De Mello insists we will feel more at ease with the people around us when we are no longer afraid of being hurt or not liked — or when we overcome the desire to impress or rid ourselves of the compulsion to explain or apologize. Nobody ever rejects us. They merely reject what they think we are. By the same token, nobody ever accepts us either. Asleep, they simply affirm the image they have constructed of us. Although being woken up is not always pleasant, it is easier to love others when we no longer identify with what we imagine they are or they imagine us to be.

He would tell friends who were hurt and troubled: "You are accustomed to think there is an 'I.' You are conditioned to think certain things affect the 'I.' It is a figment of your imagination. It is a creation of society. Liberation comes when you know there is no I to get hurt or loved or appreciated or rejected. I as a subject of 'good' and 'bad' experience is a myth which has become deeply rooted in our psyche."[6] One of de Mello's stories was entitled "Dropping the 'I' ":

Disciple: I have come to offer you my service.

Master: If you dropped the "I," service would automatically follow.

You could give all your goods to feed the poor and your body to be burned and not have love at all....

Keep your goods and abandon the "I." Don't burn your body; burn the ego. Love will automatically follow.[7]

For de Mello happiness is the goal of life, but he says that instead many experience only suffering caused by *attachment* — "happiness sought through conditions." We need to be released from this conditioning of the mind by cultivating *detachment* through a process of discernment. This ultimately leads to happiness, which is freedom. Happiness releases us from the self, whereas misery and depression bind us to the self. We are conscious of a tooth when we have a toothache, but we are not even aware we have a tooth after we have been relieved of the pain it is causing.

The Path of True Happiness

De Mello distinguishes between acquired happiness (material accumulation, academic success, career promotion, pleasures of body and mind, recognition and fame) and real happiness (a state of mind in which people experience peace, joy, contentment, love, compassion, and thanksgiving — all in one). Acquired happiness is fleeting and, as it passes from our grasp, the thirst for more intensifies. It creates suffering in the form of frustration, depression, or even suicide. While happiness cannot be purchased with money or power, it can be experienced in the here and now as well as in eternity.

He makes a careful distinction between pain and suffering. In life, pain is inevitable, part of the process of living. But if people immunize themselves against all pain, they will never grow. Pain comes from the outside and is not of a person's making. Suffering, on the other hand, arises from within and should be avoided and eliminated. It can be shocking, says de Mello, for people to discover that they themselves give expression to their suffering. In his book *Sadhana* de Mello explains:

> During a Buddhist retreat I made, we were asked to sit for a whole hour at a stretch without moving. I happened to be sitting cross-legged and the pain in my knees and back became so intense it was excruciating. I do not remember ever having suffered so much physical pain in all my life. We were supposed, during that hour, to be aware of our body sensations, moving from one part of the body to another. My awareness was wholly absorbed by the acute pain in my knees. I was sweating profusely. And I thought I should faint with the pain — until I decided not to fight it, not to run away from it,

not to desire to alleviate it, but to become aware of it, to identify with it. I broke the pain sensation up into its component
parts and I discovered, to my surprise, that it was composed
of many sensations, not just one: there was an intense burning
sensation, a pulling and tugging, a sharp, shooting sensation
that merged every now and then... and a point which kept
moving from one place to another. This point I identified as
the *pain*.... As I kept up this awareness exercise I found I
was bearing the pain quite well and even had some awareness left over for other sensations in other parts of my body.
For the first time in my life I was experiencing pain without
suffering.[8]

Suffering, then, is caused by attachment, which is the craving
for possessing (or the craving for shunning) someone or something.
As people expect to be happy according to their own models of
happiness, attachment can manifest itself in two ways: in craving
for a desired object like a new partner — or by craving to eliminate
an undesired object. For example, "I like Jane but hate Juliette.
I seek the company of Jane to make myself important." That is
attachment. But "I seek all means to push out Juliette because I
hate her age and appearance" is also attachment in de Mello's eyes
because it implies that "I believe that I will be happy when I will
have eliminated her (the undesired object)."

People become programmed through attachments in the form of
expectations toward oneself and toward others, and expectations
of others toward oneself and toward one's life. But in trying to
find meaning to their lives in this way people become only restless
and unsatisfied. What they are seeking is not happiness (joy, peace,
and contentment) but their own distorted idea of happiness, which
they keep craving for through attachments. Developing the Ignatian principle of discernment, de Mello teaches that the way out of
such psychological imprisonment is through self-observation and by
being challenged. This leads to detachment. A detached person is
free. There is joy in possessing the objects of a person's desires but

joy also when a person does not possess them. Success and failure can, therefore, be received with equal pleasure.

It is easy to equate this summary of de Mello's spirituality with the Four Noble Truths of Buddhism, to which it bears more than passing resemblance. While many point to the fact that de Mello remained at heart a Catholic priest, it is understandable why some sensed, as the years went by, that he seemed to have a closer affinity with the spirit of Eastern religions. On the opening page of one of his books, for instance, he refers to "Buddha and Jesus" as examples of "The Spiritual Teachers of humanity" who taught truth through storytelling.[9] That was what de Mello always tried to do.

In the Shadow of "The Great Soul"

Born on September 4, 1931, in Bombay (now Mumbai), Anthony de Mello was the eldest of four in a family that hailed from Goa, a former Portuguese colony. He was raised in the Roman Catholic Church and entered the Jesuit order at sixteen. Jesuits are members of the Society of Jesus, a Catholic religious order whose founder, St. Ignatius of Loyola (1491–1556), was a soldier before becoming a priest. These days they prefer to be known as "Companions of Jesus" rather than "Soldiers of Christ." Pope Benedict XVI has described Ignatius as a man who gave the first place of his life to God. St. Ignatius compiled the Spiritual Exercises, a month-long program of meditations, prayers, considerations, and contemplative practices that, to this day, help people connect their faith with their everyday lives. Jesuits are the largest male religious order in the Catholic Church, engaged in ministries in 112 nations on 6 continents. They are best known for their work in education, intellectual research, and missionary enterprise, but are also involved with social justice projects, human rights activities, and interreligious dialogue.

De Mello's first program had its roots in the fifteen-day Ignatian Retreat he made under Father Ignacio Calveras (an authority in Ignatian spirituality) during his formation years in Spain. When he returned to Bombay, he took up a teaching appointment as part of what Jesuits call a "regency." After a year, he was sent to teach English to the young novices and juniors at Vinayalaya, the mother house of the Bombay Jesuit province. Following theological formation at De Nobili College, Poona (Pune), he was ordained a priest in 1961 and then studied for a master's degree in counseling at Loyola University in Chicago. This enlarged his cultural and intellectual horizons as he mixed with free thinkers and became familiar with various schools of psychology, including Transactional Analysis and Gestalt. From Carl Rogers he learnt the concepts of acceptance (the continual attention paid to the other), empathy (the ability to feel what the other person feels), and congruence (the awareness of one's own feelings toward another). He also studied Fritz Perls's basic principle of "a continuum of awareness," later to become the center of his own approach as he set about applying these new psychological discoveries to the spiritual domain.

After studying spiritual theology at the Gregorian University in Rome, de Mello worked briefly at a mission station in rural Maharashtra and then returned to Vinayalaya as rector, where he conceived a plan to direct thirty-day Ignatian retreats for Jesuits in the manner of Ignacio Calveras. But he was not satisfied with a purely spiritual approach to personal growth, telling his groups: "We should never put a spiritual patch on a psychological wound." Emerging as a contextual theologian and one of the pioneers of the inculturation movement in India, de Mello worked closely and naturally with Hindus and Muslims. He was greatly inspired by Mahatma Gandhi, the pioneer of *satyagraha* — resistance to tyranny through mass civil disobedience — who led India to independence. At one stage, de Mello even suggested students should dress like Gandhi to get inside "the great soul."

De Mello told friends that, for him, Christ had been a person who had been true to his inner promptings, someone who had relentlessly followed his inner voice and, in that sense, should be emulated by Indian Christians. But he felt statements about the uniqueness of Christ should be understood mythologically or poetically, and not in a rationalistic or literal way. He said Jesus preached what he lived. Gandhi lived what he preached. As a person, Christ was very much alive because his teaching came from the experience of life. Gandhi was logical and reasoned. His life was, therefore, less flavored.

Finding God in All Things

I traveled to the San Francisco Bay area of California to meet a leading Jesuit educator who was a student under Anthony de Mello in those early years. At the time of our conversation, Father Joseph Daoust was president of the Jesuit School of Theology at Berkeley, which is affiliated with the Graduate Theological Union. Here students from more than forty countries are trained for ministry in many different cultural contexts. In the GTU bookshop, I came across a plaque with the words "To teach is to touch someone for life." It was to offer a clue to the secret of Tony de Mello.

Sitting in his office, with panoramic views of the Pacific coast, Father Daoust described how de Mello had tapped into a deep desire in the psyche of many Americans for a spirituality without walls. De Mello was effective at helping those with deep religious convictions as well as spiritual seekers wary of institutional religion. But wherever they happened to be in their lives, people from all backgrounds were helped by de Mello "to find God in all things." He succeeded in bringing them to a sense of the transcendent as well as to an awareness of their own interdependence both on others and on the Divine. He appealed especially to people who had rejected, were untouched by, or bored with traditional theological approaches. For de Mello, the more human you became, the more in touch you were with God. Searchers of the spiritual, haunted by the memory of disturbing religious imagery or oppressive preachers of their past, found solace in the reassuring waters of Anthony de Mello, who tossed overboard jargon that he felt had been overused or misused in religious upbringing.

Father Daoust told me that it was de Mello's wholeness, rather than his holiness, that stood out as his most tangible quality when they first met in India in 1971 at the beginning of tertianship, a six- to nine-month period of spiritual training for Jesuits at the end of their studies. "Two days later we had our first conference and in that forty-five minutes he saw through me more than anybody else had in my life," said Father Daoust. "I think he got a lot just from looking at me, as well as from what I said, which wasn't very revelatory. But he was able to get beneath it and touch into things in a very nonthreatening way. I was thirty-two at the time. I had never been in serious spiritual direction or therapy where people probed. But he immediately saw very key things that underlay some of my struggles at that time."

It was not just de Mello's psychological penetration that had been awesome but the fact that, without much help from Joseph Daoust himself, the insightful teacher had been able to connect the student's psychological struggles with his spiritual issues. "He was whole but he also made you feel the wholeness of creation and of the world's religions in yourself. That was his charism. We Westerners often dice things into 'this is psychological,' 'this is spiritual' and 'this is physical.' He did not preach against that but just did not storm those barricades. He walked away in another direction where those distinctions were less important and flowed one into the other."

The students (mostly Indian) seemed both taken aback and touched when de Mello turned up one day with a Hindu, a Muslim, and a Sikh to help lead the spiritual exercises in preparation for the thirty-day retreat. It was an interfaith celebration of God, inspired by de Mello, who could operate seamlessly without the need for major cultural gear changes. Daoust remembered the spiritual master using stories from Indian religious traditions with the same ease of manner that he drew on episodes from Christian history, though de Mello did not directly address matters of interfaith dialogue. He was not a retiring figure, but someone actively present in a way that calmed members of the group. He made them believe there was a gracious God accompanying them in addressing the issues of the day, and many felt reintegrated as a result. At times the atmosphere

took on an almost cosmic guise, uniting the sense of personal wholeness with the physical environment and the entire human race. De
Mello took delight in communicating the puzzlement of the uni-
verse. Students could go to him with a personal issue or a global
question, and de Mello had the knack of turning the problem into
a riddle that offered wisdom into how to move forward.

In Indian culture, people have traditionally touched the feet of a
guru, such as Ramana Maharshi or Ma Anandamayi. But according to Joseph Daoust, Anthony de Mello never assumed such auras
of greatness. On the contrary, he projected himself as "a very humble but very present" person. "When he was in the room, he was
impossible to ignore. But the moment was never about him but
about knowing that you were in the presence of a great friend, even
if you had just met him. Furthermore, if someone walked into the
room and met Tony for the first time in a decade, they would carry
on where they had left off."

The unmistakable humanity of Tony de Mello was always in evidence and there was never any hint of a tortured soul. He might have
faced inner struggles alone, but his demeanor suggested he must
have come through unscathed. "He was very explicitly a Jesuit, but
I think he got rid of some of the explicitness in his public persona,"
said Father Daoust. "He didn't cease being a Jesuit, but he stopped
dressing like one. He was someone who was able to transcend lines.
I got the impression that he felt many people's views of institutional
religion were projected onto God and, as a result, created fear and
anxiety in them. He got people to move beyond that thinking, not
by smashing or attacking their projections, but by telling them that
they did not need to walk that way. It was a gentle and effective
critique of institutions. On the long retreat, he told us there were
two ways to destroy a temple. You could, like Samson, push the
pillars out — and the temple comes crashing down. Or you can just
walk away and nobody will use it. Tony would always take the second rather than the first approach." In Daoust's eyes, de Mello was
the ultimate nonfundamentalist but, at the same time, not a rela-
tivist. He was in search of the living God and came in touch with

God through other people. It was a vision not unlike that of the great Jesuit writer Teilhard de Chardin, rather than a mysticism of St. John of the Cross.

During the 1970s de Mello began to promote the Eastern meditational practice of *vipassana* (seeing things as they really are) and gradually exposed himself to Buddhist spirituality, confronting his traditional theological training with existential questions. He would ask, for example, if the response of Jesus Christ to the human predicament was substantially different from that of Krishna, the Buddha or Moses, and whether Catholics should care about the differences. When he addressed a retreat for Jesuits at Loyola Hall, an Ignatian spirituality center near Liverpool, England, de Mello's sense of integration became a talking point. One of those who attended commented: "It was clear he knew what it was like being a real human being, especially on the psychological and sexual levels, rather than aspiring to the idealized human being that a good religious should be. His mix of Christianity, psychology, and Indian religious wisdom was particularly rich."

The Art of Awareness

Establishing the Institute for Pastoral Counselling and Spirituality at De Nobili College, Poona, he chose for his method the name *sadhana,* a Sanskrit word meaning "effort toward a goal" or "spiritual training," a common term in Hinduism and Buddhism. *Sadhana: A Way to God* was the title of de Mello's first paperback in 1978. The Catholic Theological Society of America hailed it as "perhaps the best book available in English for Christians on how to pray, meditate, and contemplate." In it de Mello explained how many had complained that they did not know how to pray, seemed to make little progress in their efforts, or found the discipline dull and frustrating. But the master said he always found it relatively easy to help people pray. It was legitimate to envisage prayer as an exercise that could bring fulfillment and satisfaction, but it should be entered into through the heart rather than the head. It was not about thinking. De Mello said that he had learned from a Jesuit friend who had approached a Hindu guru for initiation in the art of prayer. The guru had told him to concentrate on his breathing for five minutes: "The air you breathe is God. You are breathing God in and out. Become aware of that, and stay with that awareness." After making a theological adjustment to the guru's statement, de Mello's friend had discovered that prayer could be as simple a matter as breathing in and out. It became a profound form of spiritual nourishment.

While these "Christian Exercises in Eastern Form" were unashamedly in line with the approach of the Hindu guru, de Mello dedicated the book to the Blessed Virgin Mary, who had always been a model of contemplation: "She has been more: I am convinced that it is her intercession that has obtained for me, and for many of the people I have guided, graces in prayer that we should never have acquired otherwise."[10] *Sadhana* swiftly became everybody's prayer book and de Mello a name on everybody's lips as his reputation grew. The book's message was not so much about doing regular exercises in prayer as a way of looking at reality prayerfully. The meditations focused on silence, stillness, body sensations, thought control, and breathing sensations. There were also fantasy exercises aimed at helping people put their lives in perspective, be released from feelings of resentment, and healed from hurtful memories. One of the exercises, borrowed from a Buddhist reality meditation series, even asked readers to concentrate imaginatively on the demise of their own corpse through its nine stages of decomposition. A devotional section included more traditional forms of contemplation, such as praise, petition, and the Jesus Prayer. The objective was to undertake a journey from the external world to the interior, creating an inner peace that brought the whole person to prayer — body and soul, heart and mind, memory and imagination.

An aspect of awareness for de Mello is observing an object attentively without bringing in one's personal judgment or a desire to change or evaluate. It is the pure act of seeing things as they are. In the first volume of his book of story meditations, *The Prayer of the Frog*, he illustrates the point:

> *A woman in the grocery department of a supermarket bent down to pick up some tomatoes. At that moment she felt a sharp pain shooting down her back; she became immobilized and let out a shriek.*
>
> *A shopper standing next to her leaned over knowingly and said: "If you think tomatoes are bad, you should see the price of the fish!"*
>
> Is it Reality you are responding to or is it your assumptions about it?[11]

According to de Mello, awareness leads to the inner discovery that everything has a beginning, a moment of becoming, and an end. The world is transitory and flows like a river. This inner realization creates a freedom that is the experience of true happiness, the crowning point of the spiritual life, causing a person to marvel at creation, wonder at beings, and be grateful to God for his continuous grace. Salvation and freedom begin, then, in the here and now when life is celebrated as a wellspring of joy and love. Nothing really changes through enlightenment, but the world is seen through new eyes.

Many people around the world experienced inner transformation after reading de Mello's writings, among them Tim Pike, of Sussex, England, who was given a copy of the book *Awareness* as a birthday present. He enjoyed the wit, the flow, and the structure, and was particularly taken by the Four Steps to Wisdom. "I popped the book on the shelf and got on with life," he told me. "Three years later, after completing M. Scott Peck's *The Road Less Traveled,* I started asking myself questions about my own direction in life. I took *Awareness* back off the shelf. This time I really read and reread it, underlining significant phrases. I thought about the four steps, about detachment, and about observing myself as if I were outside myself. I became aware of feelings I did not know were there. This led me to train as a counselor — and I became a patient, too, as part of that process. I found the therapist's insights and interpretations liberating, but they were also painful, humiliating, or intensely sad at times. The truth I was learning about myself was setting me free. My own self-observations were sufficient for the change to glide in at its own pace. Sometimes it was profound, sometimes difficult. I realized that blaming others or external events could be easier than admitting the feeling was mine and in me."

Now qualified, Tim Pike counsels others as their therapist. He spends much of his time organizing groups for men who are violent toward women. "A rapport soon develops when, thanks to my counseling training, which was sparked by reading de Mello, I am able to spot their feelings and name an emotion they are acting out, such as shame or fear," Tim explained. "Their eyes widen and, leaning forward, they start to concentrate. They begin to show up on time. Some start to express themselves openly using a vocabulary and an emotional grammar that sets them free. Some learn to understand why they beat women. Others don't, but they do learn how to control themselves rather than control others.

"Liberty for the emotionally captive is what de Mello means to me."

The Holy Wanderer

As de Mello continued to be acclaimed as one of the world's foremost and original spiritual guides, some Jesuits became uneasy to the point of suspicion about his embrace of Eastern spirituality. They felt he was moving too far from his Catholic roots. The counseling and spirituality center, renamed Sadhana Institute, relocated to a villa at Lonavla, between Bombay and Poona, where its work (or perhaps more specifically de Mello) was monitored. Lonavla became an oasis for groups of religious men and women who undertook practical courses called *sadhanas*, led by de Mello and a small team. The emphasis was increasingly on talks, group therapy, role-play, and spiritual direction, rather than on meditation and contemplation. It was an intercultural approach where people from all backgrounds and religions could feel at home. Although he combined different forms of Christian spirituality in his talks, there were sometimes misgivings that the ebullient Jesuit was too fond of mixing his own oriental cocktails without the fundamental Catholic ingredients. But others, aware that de Mello's immense popularity could easily trigger jealousy and resentment within the Society of Jesus, defended the priest, whose intentions were always to foster people's inner growth and development. As de Mello acknowledges in *The Song of the Bird:*

> This book has been written for people of every persuasion, religious and nonreligious. I cannot, however, hide from my readers the fact that I am a priest of the Catholic Church. I have wandered freely in mystical traditions that are not Christian and not religious, and I have been profoundly influenced by them. It is to my Church, however, that I keep returning, for she is my spiritual home; and while I am acutely, sometimes embarrassingly, conscious of her limitations and narrowness, I also know that it is she who has formed me and made me what I am today. So it is to her that I gratefully dedicate this book.[12]

During these years, the slightly overweight, six-foot-two-inch frame of Tony de Mello was maintained through regular walking and bioenergetic disciplines. With his wavy black hair, graying at the sides, and beaming face, he looked like the picture of health. He rose early for Zen exercises and breathing awareness techniques. His teachings always flowed from a deep prayer life. There was a depth to his eyes, shielded by dark thick-rimmed spectacles with large square lenses and a look that suggested there was "something beyond." It was as though he had been to the frontiers of spirituality and made a discovery. Opinions of him, though, were rarely as united as he appears to have been as a person. Some saw him as a sage who was helping people clear psychological blockages within themselves so the current of God's love could flow freely. A few felt he was deliberately casting himself in the light of an international

Indian guru. Others dismissed such ideas, pointing out that he never held power over others but guided people with certitude and authority. De Mello, though, had a powerful personality — too powerful for some, who occasionally felt belittled by him. "He was one of the modern mystics," said an Indian Jesuit who knew him well. "He became a spiritual master naturally. He had a magnetic personality. People liked being in his company. He was offering something new. He challenged his audience to think for themselves and, if they were annoyed in the process, so be it. A mystic for him was a contemplative in close communication with God and humanity, a prophet who spoke the voice of God fearlessly. Tony had that mystical freedom to wander into different territories and take away what he found useful, which he would then pass on to others. He moved from his traditional Catholic background — although he himself would have said it was precisely because he was so deeply rooted in the church that he discovered the freedom to own his wings and fly. In his very presence and in his teaching, he would come across as a Zen master. His style could shock and jolt people. Some did not get over the experience and were permanently alienated from his teaching. But Tony was not afraid of such reactions and could be compassionate.

"If you had a meal with him, he would be joyful, cracking jokes and full of life. He was classically extrovert. Somehow he would get to the heart of a matter very quickly and not feel the need to give an elaborate response. That is the style of a Zen master, provoking you to think something else. Very often you did not get the response you were looking for with Tony. Whether in counseling, a group session, or on video, you saw that gift of awakening people. Even as a young priest, he evoked something in the congregation when he was preaching." Although his traditional Catholic upbringing was always with him, he seemed to move every fifteen minutes. In that sense he was very Buddhist. He embodied that idea of impermanence. He kept on changing and accepting whatever was beautiful. Provocation and argument were his delights:

*The devil once went for a walk with a friend. They saw a man
ahead of them stoop down and pick up something from the
ground.*

"What did that man find?" asked the friend.

"A piece of truth," said the devil.

"Doesn't that disturb you?" asked the friend.

"No," said the devil. "I shall let him make a belief out of it."

A religious belief is a signpost pointing the way to truth, remarks
de Mello in one of his books. When you cling to the signpost, you
are prevented from moving toward the truth because you think you
have found it already.[13]

The Public and Private Worlds

People spoke of the smiling Buddha, but they talked of the Laugh-
ing Tony, whose mirth was always in abundance. He honed the
skills of performing but was always true to himself. He did, not,
however, like to be put on a pedestal, though (like Henri Nouwen)
he was never dazzled by the spotlight. One writer, Anand Nayak,
has speculated: "A spiritual master, having become a master, loses
the simplicity in life to learn things with others by becoming one
among others. I wonder if Tony was not sometimes victim to this
tendency. He certainly had a wonderful charisma to enliven conversations, group discussions, and group therapies. Evidently, nobody
else could do as well as he did. But one also felt that he had the
need to be the center of attention. One did not see Tony working
with others or making himself one amongst others, or trying to find
solutions in discussion with others. He was invariably the master in
all situations."[14]

De Mello liked to be in control and therefore was not always at
ease when he was being challenged. At one of his retreats, he was
asked about hell. The audience expected a serious consideration of

an important topic. De Mello merely replied that, according to the Christian tradition, people should believe in hell. But he said God was compassionate. "I suppose God would have a hell but he would forget to put the heater on," he laughed. While watching a film as he hosted a pan-America satellite conference from New York, I once noticed how a number of contributors were asking penetrating questions from their various university bases. But instead of providing the responses they deserved, de Mello would hesitate, dismiss the points, laugh, and move on. Not everyone might have been amused, for it appeared rather disingenuous. In his defense, friends say he would always read behind the questions, aware of what they were not asking or what they were implying. But that hardly excuses his elusiveness in fielding pertinent questions, however awkward he found them.

But as he grew older, Tony de Mello seemed to care less about what people thought about him as he repeatedly refocused his spiritual vision. Although he kept up a public display of self-assurance, there were private periods of inner darkness, not uncommon to followers of the mystical path. In 1986, he experienced a state of despair, fright, and loneliness in which he felt abandoned by God and the world. It was as though nobody could reach him. Yet the following year (during a seminar the week before he died) he seemed to be on the point of a new liberation as he spoke of a grateful heart never being unhappy. He told his listeners that when they woke up every morning, they should remind themselves that they might not see tomorrow, and then they would enjoy each day. By thinking of death, they would start to live.

The day before he died, he wrote: "I find the whole of my interest is now focused on something else, on the 'world of the Spirit,' and I see everything else as trifling and so irrelevant . . . never before in my life have I felt so happy, so free. . . . "[15] His death of a heart attack on June 2, 1987, was (like Merton's) treated initially as suspicious. He was discovered lying on the floor in a fetal position with his thumb in his mouth. He had just arrived in New York to begin a six-month tour conducting various *sadhana* programs in North America.

Bombshells and Belly Laughs

Some Jesuits remain convinced that, at the time of his death, de Mello had moved far from the religion of his birth. To find out more, I flew to Spain to meet Father Carlos Vallés, SJ, who, at the age of twenty-four, went to India as a Jesuit missionary and got to know de Mello well. He wrote *Unencumbered by Baggage,*[16] the first personal portrait of de Mello, and later authored *Diez años después* (Ten years after),[17] which, in the absence of an analytical biography of de Mello, outlined what the author claimed was de Mello's "gradual distancing from Catholic orthodoxy."

At his home in a suburb of Madrid, Carlos Vallés told me that Tony de Mello had undoubtedly been the right person with the right program at the right time for the world of spiritual seekers. "His personal charisma attracted both individuals and crowds with the same appeal, originality, charm, wit, clarity, courage, informality, unconventionality, humor, and depth that challenged established uses and promised quick and steady personal growth to all at whatever stage in their lives," he said. "De Mello was a master of the parable, the joke, the humorous quip, the risqué remark, the wisdom story that made others laugh and think, and pointed to unexpected results with a disarming smile. His gift as a communicator, his total commitment to his task at hand, and his ability to obtain collaborators to help with his courses and to organize his public talks had been at the root of a deep and wholesome influence."

Vallés retired to Spain after spending fifty years in India. From his home he runs a virtual parish on the Internet (*www.carlosvalles.com*), where he professes to continue de Mello's teachings in his own way. In his view, de Mello talked only about God as a matter of language to connect with his readers and listeners, not as a personal conviction. Father Vallés claimed de Mello realized he could not speak of prayer to Christians without mentioning the name of God and, therefore, made references to the divine for their sake and not his own.

"In Lonavla we used to quip that we were always at the mercy of Tony's last visit to the USA," said Father Vallés. "He nourished himself in America. I fancy to think that his approach of self-worth, of continued growth, of living the present, of constant awareness, of contact with the senses, of optimism, of detachment, of de-conditioning ourselves, of openness, of living without masks, of being aware of our feelings and trusting them above our thoughts, of freedom of guilt, of deep relationships, of welcoming things as they are and life as it comes (in a word, of inner freedom in joy and hope) is the timely and providential message for the shaping of a new mentality in the world-in-crisis we are living in. It was and is a spirituality for our times."

But Father Vallés revealed that, when he made the nine-month *sadhana* course, de Mello announced that he had "some bomb-shells" ready for us, built up expectations for them, delivered them with all the emphasis at his disposal (which was considerable), and based his whole course on them: "The bombshell was the core Buddhist doctrine that there is no Self. There is no person, no identity, no 'I,' nothing behind this organism, nothing to carry 'me' over to eternity, as there is no 'me.' All this was couched in traditional and familiar examples and images. He told me in a private meeting: 'This is my secret, Carlos. I preach pure Buddhism. But quoting the Bible constantly, and setting up Jesus as a model.' And he then gave one of his characteristic belly laughs. But his central point in our *sadhana* was that there is no Self and therefore no person after death. It was fundamental to his teaching at that moment and radically opposed to any Christian view. The fact that not a single, full-scale, critical biography of de Mello has been published since his death more than twenty years ago seems to confirm that those who knew him were reluctant to publish what they knew about him and chose silence rather than exposure."

The Crucible of Experience

Others, however, strongly refute this and think it improbable that de Mello died a Buddhist. Among them is Anand Nayak, a former Jesuit from India who learned *sadhana* from de Mello and is now professor of missiology and comparative religions at the University of Fribourg, Switzerland. Professor Nayak, who promotes de Mello's teachings in a number of countries and conducts regular *sadhana* courses, has written a book about de Mello's life and spirituality.[18] He said that while de Mello read widely about different religions, gained a technical knowledge about many of them, and conversed with their leaders, he did not quote other religions specifically, even though he made use of them in his writings and lectures. He told me: "Tony brought all teachings to the crucible test of his personal experience. If it was meaningful for him, then that was sufficient. He never spoke about things that were not meaningful for his own personal life. A pure academic attitude was not in him. So it is difficult to see him as a Buddhist. It is true, however, that his teachings resemble very much those of the Theravada School of Buddhism, but all the great religions have the same spiritual model, akin to the Four Noble Truths. He remained a true Catholic, a Jesuit faithful to the church and to his order. Having understood the real meaning of prayer, Mass, and the breviary, he would not bind himself — with guilt feelings — to such practices and traditions. He loved to pray and to say the Mass. His last Mass, which he celebrated in public two weeks before his death, incorporated all the participants who had gathered for a refresher course of *sadhana*. I am sure he remained until the end a convinced priest and religious. His Catholic identity had grown to such an extent that he felt at home wherever there was life and light. 'A spirituality that is good, should be good for all,' he would say. This annoyed some of the church hierarchy. But he said he drew on some of the values from other religions, not because of their place in those systems, because they were values for all. He also rejected religious values in which he found no meaning."

Father José Javier Aizpún, who was superior of the Jesuit community at Lonavla when de Mello died, had the responsibility of sorting through de Mello's possessions. Among them, he found a carbon copy of a response de Mello had typed to a religious sister who had been on a course but had subsequently wanted to find out what de Mello really felt and believed about Christ. In substance, the reply stated that Jesus Christ would always be his "Bhagavan" (meaning Lord, the object of a devotee's loving devotion). No one else could ever take that place in his life, he told her. But the theological articulations of two natures and one person, and the Christological formulations, made little sense to him. "That was part of what, regrettably, was a typical attitude and reaction of Tony," said Father Aizpún. "He dismissed too casually what did not fit in his own scheme of things. He knew his textbook theology quite well but I suspect he never went deeply into any of it."

Father Aizpún also came across a small statue of Our Lady, which de Mello had kept for much of his life. Among the papers, written in his own hand and signed by him, was the formula of consecration to Our Lady that he had made in the novitiate. "His tender devotion to Mary was no secret. He freely shared that with the groups. If asked how that squared with his often iconoclastic views on religiosity, he would say that part of a person's search for wisdom is the freedom not to be totally consistent with one's views or formulations. Perhaps there was something of the Indian, oriental mind in that: not either this or that but both this and that."

"Unconventional and Inconsistent"

De Mello was upset when he heard people remarking that he had lost his faith in the Eucharist, said Father Aizpún. In his last years de Mello tended not to participate in the daily Eucharist of a group, except on special occasions. But he valued the Mass, saying that "if the Lord had not given it to the church, the church would have had to invent it." De Mello never seems to have expressed his faith in the common, expected way. To be unconventional was second nature to him. But some people became irritated by de Mello's inconsistency. He used to boast to audiences that they might hear him express views in direct opposition to what he had said at a conference the previous year. For some of his *chelas* (devoted disciples) this could be extremely disconcerting. But his temperament was to provoke people into thinking for themselves rather than living on borrowed ideas.

"The end of his life was not a final point of arrival but simply another stage in the journey when he happened to die," said Father Aizpún. "Yet, for all the new discoveries, there was also an element of rediscovering the past in a new light. Temperamentally when he saw a new light, it occupied not just center stage but the entire stage, displacing everything else. He did not seem concerned about trying to integrate all the lights before him. It was more important to live by the truth as it was perceived at any given moment. So there was an immense subjectivism in the search and opinions of Anthony de Mello. When he was interested in the Spiritual Exercises of St. Ignatius, the only author worth reading was Calveras. When he became involved in counseling, Carl Rogers became his guru. When he later discovered Krishnamurti, there was no thinker in the world comparable to him.

"His room had a very good collection of books by and on Krishnamurti and he began to expound his teachings eloquently, fervently, intelligently, and somewhat one-sidedly, as he always did. On the other hand, he was very intelligent, and it did not take him long to discover the flaws. By that time he had probably discovered another wisdom figure. I take with a big grain of salt his profession of new faith as well as his disclaimers of old beliefs, though I still maintain that he was far too casual in treating matters of traditional faith and Christian practice."

Father Aizpún now lives in Argentina, where there are fervent admirers of de Mello. But as he pointed out: "I go for Mass every Sunday to a church in one of the slum areas (*villas miseria*) of Buenos Aires. To the people there, struggling to survive, Tony is far beyond their comprehension, if not totally irrelevant. That is perhaps the greatest limitation of Tony's writings. I wonder if they make sense to people outside a certain elite. But isn't that the case with the vast majority of writers? To that, Tony would say, 'It may be so, it may not be so. Who knows?'"

The Vatican Investigation

It was not until more than a decade after Anthony de Mello's death that the prefect of the Congregation for the Doctrine of the Faith in Rome, Cardinal Joseph Ratzinger (who later became Pope Benedict XVI) ordered an investigation into the Indian's writings. The Notification stated that, while de Mello's books could be helpful in achieving self-mastery and a sense of inner liberation, there was a progressive distancing from the essential contents of Christian belief: "In place of the revelation that has come in the person of Jesus Christ, he substitutes an intuition of God without form or image, to the point of speaking of God as a pure void. To see God it is enough to look directly at the world. Nothing can be said about God; the only knowing is unknowing. To pose the question of his existence is already nonsense."[19] While de Mello demonstrated an appreciation for Jesus, of whom he had declared himself to be a disciple, some might get the impression that for him Christ was a master alongside others.

The Notification continued: "The only difference from other men is that Jesus is 'awake' and fully free, while others are not. Jesus is not recognized as the Son of God but simply as the one who teaches us that all people are children of God. In addition the author's statements on the final destiny of man give rise to perplexity. At one point he speaks of a 'dissolving' into the impersonal God, as salt dissolves into water. On various occasions, the question of destiny after death is declared to be irrelevant; only the present life should be of interest. With respect to this life, since all evil is simply ignorance, there are no objective rules of morality. Good and evil are simply mental evaluations imposed upon reality.

"Consistent with what has been presented, one can understand how, according to the author, any belief or profession of faith whether in God or Christ cannot but impede one's personal access to truth."[20]

Bishops were ordered to intercept the sale of de Mello's books and ensure that his teachings did not circulate in their dioceses.

Warnings were placed inside paperbacks already on sale (only making potential readers even more curious). While the writings were not ultimately outlawed, some editions were supplemented with a caution: "The books of Father Anthony de Mello were written in a multi-religious context to help the followers of other religions, agnostics and atheists in their spiritual searching and they were not intended by the author as manuals of instruction of the Catholic faithful in Christian doctrine or dogma."

I have seen a copy of a letter, written by Cardinal Ratzinger on July 23, 1998, and sent to the presidents of the Conferences of Bishops. In it, the prefect states that, following "reports coming to this Congregation," de Mello's texts have been examined and found to contain statements and tendencies "which lead to a relativizing of every affirmation of faith and thus to religious indifferentism." He explains that "in order to safeguard the good of the Christian faithful," the Notification will be published in an Italian newspaper with an explanatory article. Cardinal Ratzinger requests that the presidents forward the Notification to bishops, asking them to make it known "to the Catholic people entrusted to their care." He goes on: "Furthermore, if there are publishing houses in your country which have printed these books, the Bishops are asked to contact them and ensure that the texts not be reprinted. With respect to volumes already printed, opportune and prudent measures should be undertaken so that they be withdrawn from sale, or at the very least, that copies of the Notification and above-mentioned explanatory article be inserted into every copy before sale."

"A Faulty Interpretation"

While some Catholic bookshops dutifully obeyed, removing de Mello's books from their shelves as if they were about to explode, elsewhere the Jesuit's writings actually began selling in even greater numbers. Neither the Roman Catholic hierarchy nor the Jesuits in India took any steps to prevent people from buying de Mello's works, although, in true Ignatian fashion, they recommended that he be read "with discernment." But they did not attempt to defend de Mello publicly.

However, in terms of accuracy and its overall perception of de Mello, the Notification was painstakingly and rigorously challenged, notably by Anand Nayak, who claimed that, while he did not question the right of the church to issue warnings for the good of the faithful or for its teaching body to determine right or wrong, "of the texts adduced to warn of the danger de Mello's writings presented to the Catholic faithful, there was not one that could rightly be used against Father de Mello." The Notification was "based on a faulty comprehension and interpretation of the texts. . . . Those who sit so close, morally, but also physically, to the seat of infallibility cannot venture to destroy the name and fame of an illustrious spiritual master with a document riddled with faults."[21] These included decontextualizing de Mello's words, misunderstanding his approach, which was in line with the language of the Christian mystical tradition, and citing from books falsely attributed to de Mello that contained notes taken down at conferences or from broadcast talks into which, said Nayak, the real authors had injected their own ideas. De Mello had not preached anything counter to the Christian message or Christian traditions. Far from distancing himself from the Roman Catholic Church, he had introduced a new language, new concepts, and new approaches to connect with modern people.

Describing de Mello as a "fire-maker from the East," Anand Nayak said that, far from being a danger to the church, he was a prophetic and mystical teacher whose works had brought immense help and healing to vast numbers. He was one of those rare spiritual masters who knew how to speak to a world in which more than 80 percent of the population had given up the regular practice of faith. De Mello introduced "a new taste and flavor" to the Christian message, making the search for God an adventure. He incorporated religious concepts and themes into his teachings, not to fuel theological debate, but to help free people from fear and anguish "in order to lighten their burden created through imaginary and structural conditions and to give people a taste for life and the joy of living." As de Mello's spirituality was embedded in the common ground of human existence, it could not be limited to a set of people or cultures. De Mello's spiritual method made people come out of their protective shells and "praise God in unison."[22]

"Double Religious Belonging"

As with all popular and influential spiritual authors, who move beyond boundaries and cannot be completely fathomed, there are sometimes attempts to control or contain, even after their deaths. But people of paradox resist definition and, while sometimes an enigma even to themselves, they often possess an inner security and freedom that propels them beyond the need for justification or condemnation.

In the study of contemporary spirituality, there is greater debate these days about the practice of "double religious belonging." Just as some "world citizens" feel at home in different countries and cultures, yet remain rooted in their own, so there have been calls for more "world believers," people with deep roots in one faith who are also able to relate to religions other than their own. This transcending of religious boundaries is known as "double religious belonging." As Ursula King has pointed out, the Japanese may practice ancient Shinto beliefs for marriage but turn to Buddhist rites at the time of death. African converts to Christianity and Islam might continue to take part in ancestral worship or maintain a belief in witchcraft. Some Hindus worship their own gods and goddesses as well as having deep devotion to Jesus Christ. De Mello would have undoubtedly agreed with King's analysis:

> Double religious belonging can be spiritually sustaining and helpful for one's life, and is probably on the increase. To encourage double belonging and strengthen it further, the world needs more people who are *spiritually* multi-lingual and

multi-focused. This is not arguing for relativism, but for true relationality between different faith perspectives and members of different faiths. In order to nurture such dialogue, it has to be asked how far religions remain closed systems or are open to outside influences. No genuine encounter can develop between systems that remain closed to each other. Yet a mere peaceful coexistence of religions, however noble, is no longer enough today. There must be a further evolution of religions themselves, in pursuit of their highest spiritual ideals, and in response to the world's greatest needs.[23]

Spirituality for Anthony de Mello was always a process of waking up, and his message of inner liberation could not be more germane to these times. He stresses that all mystics are united in the belief that all is ultimately well. "Though everything is a mess, all is well," de Mello writes. "Strange paradox, to be sure. But, tragically, most people never get to see that all is well because they are asleep. They are having a nightmare.... "[24]

Although his followers in India were largely priests and members of religious orders, in the United States (a country which, ironically, sent numerous Christian missionaries to India) it was largely lay people who comprised his audiences. De Mello believed the East-West exchange could be mutually enriching from a range of cultural, spiritual, and theological perspectives — much like the thinking of Merton, whom he read and quoted. It was in America that de Mello found his most appreciative listeners. As a character in the award-winning film *Gandhi*, puts it: "We Westerners have a weakness for these spiritually inclined men of India." In a time of recession, perhaps there are particular lessons to learn from his "one-minute wisdom." After all, de Mello believed that calamities could bring growth and enlightenment, moving people one step nearer to living fully in the here and now.

De Mello is a spiritual master for all ages because he shows that, no matter the historical era or the human situation, people suffer because they are victims of our own conditioning. They key to inner transformation is awareness, and there can be few spiritual locksmiths more accomplished than Anthony de Mello.

A disciple once complained, "You tell us stories, but you never reveal their meaning to us."

Said the master, "How would you like it if someone offered you fruit and masticated it before giving it to you?" No one can find *your* meaning for you. Not even the master.[25]

SIX

Befriending the Soul
The Landscapes of John O'Donohue

I would love to live
Like a river flows,
Carried by the surprise
Of its own unfolding.[1]

"All around us are these black, bleak mountains which are incredibly intense," said John O'Donohue as he guided me through a small glacial valley on the west coast of Ireland. "Today the light is very low so the fog is covering the mountains. When the fog is there, half of them are missing. But, in some sense, that is the duty of the imagination: to help us connect with that which is invisible but is actually very close."

John O'Donohue was an Irish philosopher and poet whose books synthesizing the spiritual wisdom of the Celtic world with European philosophy turned him into an international phenomenon as the twentieth century drew to a close. Described variously as a spiritual bard, a priestly troubadour, and a prophet for anxious times, he crafted lush prose to nourish readers with a spiritual hunger in the postmodern crisis of belonging, an audience weary of consumerist living and often disillusioned with institutional forms of religion. He sought to rescue prayer from conventional forms of piety and return it graciously to the ancient narrative of the soul. People said his words brought them closer to themselves.

Born on New Year's Day in 1956 in County Clare, John O'Donohue was one of four children. He grew up in the Burren, a name whose roots lie in an Irish word, *bhoireann*, meaning a stony place.

John would tell friends that he thought his father, a farmer and stonemason, "was in that realm of the mystically sacred." Both John's father and uncle had respect for the old oral traditions of Ireland, and for language, poetry, and music. All talking in the house took place in the evenings. There wasn't a television set in the family home, only gentle smoke from the fire.

At the age of twelve, John became a boarder at St. Mary's College, Galway, and later trained for the Catholic priesthood at a seminary in Maynooth. After his ordination in 1981, John served for nearly two decades as a parish priest in both Clare and Conamara, where he cultivated his pastoral gift for the care of the dying. But there were always tensions with what he saw as the confining rigors of Irish Catholicism. Through his ministry with parishioners, he tried "to refine their fingers... so that they could undo so much of the false netting crippling their own spirits."[2] O'Donohue spent four years at Tübingen University, Germany, studying philosophy and theology. His doctorate on the German philosopher Georg Wilhelm Friedrich Hegel (1770–1831), earned him a *summa cum laude* in 1990. A book on Hegel was published three years later, followed by a collection of poems, *Echoes of Memory*. On his return to Ireland O'Donohue requested permission to serve the church on a part-time basis in order to write. But his bishop refused and insisted he go back to parish life. O'Donohue's position became untenable.

A literary agent, impressed by O'Donohue's radio talks about his poems, suggested he might like to commit to paper his ideas about the lasting imprint of Celtic culture and mythology in Ireland. A new chapter began to unfold as the poet-philosopher set to work on *Anam Ċara* (Gaelic for "Soul Friend"). It proved a painstaking project but, on publication, soared onto the bestseller lists, even surpassing two books on Princess Diana in the process. The Indian-American philosopher Deepak Chopra called *Anam Ċara* "a work that will be a powerful and life-transforming experience for those who read it." The book was repeatedly printed and the Catholic theologian from the Emerald Isle found himself thrust into the limelight as he became a speaker of international renown in Europe and the United States. Americans liked to cast O'Donohue as a "priest from the wilderness" but he would have none of it. He was first and foremost a scholar who needed solitude in order to write.

"A Theater of Light and Shape"

My journey across the heart of Ireland to find O'Donohue's west coast hideaway was long and serpentine. As our meeting had been arranged by a third party, I had not managed to speak to the writer directly. A number of telephone messages remained unanswered and I began to wonder if he had changed his mind. But as he was traveling back from the American lecture circuit, I guessed he might be sleeping off the jet lag, so I kept alert to the possibility of an encounter with a man I very much wanted to interview. There were few signposts to guide me under the brooding skies of Conamara, and his home was impossible to locate without the help of local people. But eventually I drew up outside the granite house. I still recall the look of amazement on his bearded face as he opened the door. At the time O'Donohue was on the point of leaving the priesthood and did not want to be questioned about it. He agreed to speak to me so long as I did not mention his holy orders. It was a sensitive negotiation: he did not like the idea of the priesthood being "marketed by the media," especially as he was no longer in a parish. He was, after all, being interviewed as an author.

O'Donohue suggested we take a walk before dusk and seemed much more at home in the great outdoors. For him, external and internal landscapes were all of a piece. Around us were huge rocks — "tabernacles of silence and memory" — abandoned randomly across fields. "Thousands and thousands and thousands of years ago a glacier came down from these mountains," he told me. "In a way, in some pristine form, the echo blast of the rocks breaking away from the glacier somehow still shrouds them. The rhythm of this place is very intense. There is a great fluency and movement. Even though I live here on my own, I am never lonely because, if I look out the window, it is a constantly changing theater of light and shape. There is no landscape I know that is dependent on light as Conamara is. It's a landscape too without many walls or frontiers so, in a certain sense, it resists categories and there is an incredible vulnerability in it. Anything that is to happen to you *can* happen to you in a place like this because the protection is so meager and thin."

A lake ahead of us suddenly came into view while, all around, the moorland seemed on the verge of rising into spring color. Animals and birds presented their own choreography to this dance of nature. O'Donohue said the sheep were ubiquitous and "almost fearless," with no respect for gravity. He had built walls, up to six feet high, to try to keep neighbors' sheep away from his property. "I have seen some of them just stand back, take one glimpse at me, then look at the wall and go right over." There were hordes of rabbits, which were all out in the road by early morning. He found the young ones "really beautiful." There were also crows and ravens — "haunted kind of creatures" — and magpies. "At the moment I am feeding a wildcat, seven ravens, and six to eight magpies. There is major music when the food appears outside." Cows, calves, the occasional fox, and "really beautiful" birds completed the orchestra of local wildlife. "Swallows turn up from faraway countries around this time every year to go nesting. They know exactly which holes between the stones and the shed to go nesting in. This place is bog, which is essentially decayed forest. It is alive with all kinds of creatures which have their own kind of geography and their own instinct."

The local landscape constantly ruptured the traditional walls of thought or images that he worked with. It was a subversive kind of landscape with a bleakness that haunted and inspired at the same time. His God, too, was wild. O'Donohue said he believed that behind the exterior appearance of our everyday lives, eternal destiny was at work. The awakening of the human spirit was a homecoming but, ironically, familiarity bred apathy. It was a subtle form of human alienation. He liked to quote Hegel, who said that the familiar, precisely because it was familiar, was not known. Friendships, relationships, even our homes, could become anaesthetized through the mechanism of familiarization. For O'Donohue, the familiar was a façade that caused us to tame, control, and ultimately forget the mystery, the otherness, the "fecund turbulence of the unknown which it masks."[3] People found it difficult to awaken to their inner world when their lives had become numbed. It was not always easy to discover something new and adventurous within, even though everything necessary for the journey had already been given. People were strangers to their deepest depths but, by owning the shadowed light of the soul world, they could take the first step toward waking up within. There were certainly shades of de Mello and Merton in what he said. Complacency and familiarity could have a stranglehold, but once people began to sense the mystery and magic of themselves they would realize that they were not helpless owners of a lifeless existence, but guests gifted with blessings and possibilities.

After he moved to Conamara, he began renovating a small house which had thick walls "made out of the stone of the place." He told me that it was the wilderness of the area that had attracted him. "I find myself very at home here. I suppose I came to write really and to follow the old path which is kind of haunting me. I absolutely feel I belong here. Belonging for me is never to do with easy, complacent sheltering but in some sense about belonging to the darkness and danger of the old rhythm. I think this landscape is essentially about transience and about death. I feel this is a very truthful place."

"The Great Tapestry of the Spirit"

"Belonging" is a powerful word in O'Donohue's vocabulary. He sees the hunger to belong as being at the vulnerable heart of human nature. The ancient and eternal values of human life — truth, unity, goodness, justice, beauty, and love — are expressions of true belonging. The thirst to belong is the longing to bridge the gulf that exists between isolation and intimacy. Distance, he says, awakens longing, while closeness is belonging. From an early age, O'Donohue had been sensitive to the absence of Irish people from their own country as a result of emigration to the United States. He had worked in America as a nineteen-year-old and met an eighty-five-year-old man from his home village who had left Ireland when he was a teenager but never returned. O'Donohue observed that, physically, the octogenarian was in America, but psychologically he had remained in North Clare. The old man could remember the names of fields, pathways, stones, trees "in camera-precise detail." O'Donohue said he recognized during his travels in the States that it must have been "a wrenching thing" for Irish immigrants to have been absent from their own place in a totally different kind of world.

Something within each person cries out for belonging, he writes. Status, achievement, and possessions may bring their own pleasures, but without a true sense of belonging, people's lives are empty and futile. Like the tree that puts its roots deep into the clay, each person needs the anchor of belonging to bend with the storms and keep moving toward the light. Each person tells a unique story of experiences and feelings, but each soul, being ancient and eternal, longs to belong, weaving that person into "the great tapestry of spirit" that connects everything everywhere:

> In this post-modern world the hunger to belong has rarely been more intense, more urgent. With many of the ancient, traditional shelters now in ruins, it is as if society has lost the art of fostering community. Consumerism propels us toward an ever more lonely and isolated existence. As consumerism numbs our longing, our sense of belonging becomes empty and cold. And although technology pretends to unite us, more often than not all it delivers are simulated images that distance us from our lives. The "global village" has no roads or neighbors; it is a faceless, impersonal landscape from which all individuality has been erased. Our politicians seem devoid of imagination and inspiration, while many of the keepers of the great religious traditions now appear to be little more than frightened functionaries. In a more uniform culture, the

management skills they employ would be efficient and successful. In a pluralistic and deeply fragmented culture, they are unable to speak to the complexities of our longings.[4]

Here one can hear echoes of Merton (and, to a lesser extent, the more diplomatic Nouwen). It is in this existential void that O'Donohue mines deep within the Celtic imagination to enrich his thinking on the *anam ċara*. While acknowledging (in the spirit of Nouwen) that no one person or place can ever quell the restlessness of the human heart, he nonetheless sees this "soul friendship" as a bond that neither space nor time can harm. It awakens an "eternal echo of love" in the hearts of the friends as they enter into a circle of intimate belonging. In the Celtic world, the *anam ċara* is the person to whom you can reveal the hidden intimacies of your life, a friendship transcending all categories or conventions. In the early Celtic church, a teacher, companion, or spiritual guide was called an *anam ċara*. O'Donohue sees Celtic spirituality as a constellation for the times. People lost in "hungry transparency" desperately need a new and gentle light where the soul can shelter and reveal its ancient belonging. Again, O'Donohue is strikingly reminiscent of Nouwen when he describes cosmic loneliness as being the root of all inner loneliness. The presence and shelter of love can transfigure loneliness, but nobody can hurt you as deeply as the one you love. When you allow "the Other" into your life, you open yourself to vulnerability. Patterns of behavior can change dramatically, with rancor and resentment swiftly replacing a sense of belonging and affection.

But the soul needs love as urgently as the body requires air, notes O'Donohue. The more people love and allow themselves to be loved, the closer they come to the kingdom of the eternal. We are sons and daughters of both darkness and light. Whereas Nouwen speaks in terms of converting loneliness into solitude, hostility into hospitality, and illusion into prayer, O'Donohue settles for other polarities. Through love, fear can change into courage, emptiness can become plenitude, distance can turn into intimacy. The *anam*

ċara experience allows a friendship a certain guarantee against separation. If two friends break through the barriers of persona and
egoism to the soul level, the unity of their souls will not easily
sever, says O'Donohue. When the soul is awakened, physical space
is transfigured. Even across long distances, these friends can stay
attuned to each other and sense the flow of each other's lives:

> In Celtic tradition the *anam ċara* was not merely a metaphor
> or ideal. It was a soul bond which existed as a recognized
> and admired social construct. It altered the meaning of iden-
> tity and perception. When your affection is kindled, the world
> of your intellect takes on a new tenderness and compassion.
> The *anam ċara* brings epistemological integration and heal-
> ing. You look and see and understand differently. Initially this
> can be disruptive and awkward, but it gradually refines your
> sensibility and transforms your way of being in the world.
> Most fundamentalism, greed, violence and oppression can be
> traced back to the separation of idea and affection. For too
> long we have been blind to the cognitive riches of feeling and
> the affective depth of ideas.[5]

In everyone's life, then, there is a deep need for a soul friend, a
relationship in which you can be understood as you are without
the need for mask or pretension. Where you are understood, you
are at home. Understanding nourishes belonging. When you really
feel understood, you are free to release yourself into the trust of
another's soul. It is precisely in the awakening and exploring of this
inner landscape that the mystery and kindness of the divine can be
experienced.

"An Undeniable Festival"

" 'Spacious' is the first word that comes to me for John's friendship
and for his nature," said Irish film producer Lelia Doolan. "The
image it carries is of a large, free, open-hearted, generous, radiant,
vulnerable man." Lelia and John first met in the 1980s, but it was

not until 1991 and a campaign over Mullaghmore mountain in the Burren that they found themselves allies "both in that struggle and then in an almost continuous conversation over everything under the sun that developed during the following years." The country-man's initial wariness melted into complete trust once a rapport was established and the pots of discussion and inquiry began to simmer. After that, there was no withholding his full trust and hospitable openness. For a man of great intellectual sophistication, he was also a person of "lovely simplicity," always testing his ability to live fully in the moment and to accept whatever consequences of loneliness and darkness accompanied it.

Lelia Doolan sensed that, even in his later years, O'Donohue still had a great deal of the boy about him. More often than not, he was a wholly light-hearted and affectionate companion, full of hilarious and frequently risqué jokes, retold with panache and followed by shouts of his own uproarious laughter, which she found to be an especially amiable characteristic. Whenever he was amused, there followed "a stupendous gale of laughter," which infected everyone in the room. His mother, Josie, and members of his family had the same full-throated laugh. Encounters between them and friends frequently resulted in "paroxysms of helpless and lengthy falling about."

He could dress with a dash of style and color, was partial to a good steak, a pint of stout, and a plump cigar, not to mention hours of speculative conversation on every conceivable topic, from art and politics to matters of eternity and the cultivation of a vegetable garden. An evening in his company, at the top of his form, was "an undeniable festival."

As Lelia Doolan reflected on John, she found herself flanked by two photographs of him. One depicted him standing in the open countryside that was his source and true home; the other featured the writer at his desk, pen in hand, musing a line into life, "french-polishing a poem."[6] The lake and bog land stretched out beyond the windows. Around the desk and on the window sills were icons of his rich life: wildflowers in a vase, a small Cézanne-like painting of country cottages, a tall blue glass bottle, reshaped stones, a green candle, a small Indian Buddha statue, a slender figure carved from bog oak, a coffee mug, along with the usual scatter of books and papers. At the corner of the desk lay volume 1 of the Sermons and Treatises of his great guide and fellow mystic, Meister Eckhart.

"The clock says 3:30 in the afternoon — it wouldn't surprise me to hear a tone poem or a melodious tune wending its way through the surrounding air," said Lelia. "This scene is attentive and workmanlike, just as the one outdoors is of rhythmic, energetic presence. And of course, they are not everything — just the first hints of someone who was rooted but who was also a medium between seen and unseen worlds, a threshold into deeper layers of surprise and meaning for anyone he came across. In the bare Conamara landscape, he found an astringent sanctuary and nurture for the work of writing and reflecting which came between his ventures into lecturing, speaking, and being in public."

The private John O'Donohue relished not only Wagner, Mozart, Beethoven, Richard Strauss (notably *Ein Heldenleben*), and the finest opera singers but also the great jazz trumpeters and blues singers like Nina Simone. In New York you might well run into him at a jazz gig. He liked Van Morrison and country music — in fact, anything unusual or songs that had good lyrics. He turned up at concerts, museums, art galleries, and bookshops. In film, he gloried in the work of Kieslowski, Kiarostami, and Tarkovsky, as well as European and independent American directors. He had a soft spot for the legendary television series *The Virginian,* which he and his brothers had watched in a neighbor's home as youngsters as they did not then have television in their home. When he was at home in Conamara, John used to watch repeats at lunchtime and admit shyly to his nostalgic addiction for its moral certitudes.

"His day-to-day conversation was informal and always original," Lelia Doolan recalled. "He would describe saying a Mass, attending to a sacrament, giving a homily, or preparing a lecture, as 'doing a gig.' And he referred to people as 'the humans.' When asked how he was feeling, he'd almost invariably say, as if it came as a complete surprise: 'I'm not too — depressed!' And, when asked how some big event had gone, he'd admit: 'I think we got away with it!' He was a man for the warm affection of a great bear hug and for giving and sending 'major hugs' when arriving or departing. In spite of his great stature, he was immensely graceful, either striding in rhythmic balance across the wide landscapes of the Burren or bending to speak to another person with reverential care."

For anyone with a heart as large and loving as John O'Donohue's, there were also times of sorrow and desolation, but he always understood and could ruefully admit, like Leonard Cohen, that it was the flaw in everything that let the light in. It made him a believable fellow traveler, said Lelia Doolan: "The really startling moment was when he spoke in public, his voice, with its unaffected accent, carrying his message for a time of change and uncertainty. His profound grasp of philosophy and theology provided the subject matter, the structure, and the concepts, but it was his genius with the play of language and ideas that turned these into accessible, poetic, and merciful possibilities for his listeners. There was something mesmerizing and trancelike in his words that made them soar. I often saw people in a dreamlike state declaring themselves revitalized when they emerged after one of his talks.

"Just as in *Anam Cara,* his intellectual powers and the rigor of a brilliant, disciplined mind were obvious, but there was also, and above all that, a welcoming kindness and an understanding of the goodness of poor humans and their frailty. I think it was this benevolence that drew so many people, often people who no longer had any time for institutional religion, to pay attention to a prospect of beauty, of belonging, of an echoing eternity that they had almost abandoned."

"A Macrocosmological Anthem"

The Irish spiritual singer Nóirín Ní Riain accompanied O'Donohue on his lecture tours. They met in a New York hotel in October 1997 as they embarked on a two-week tour to promote *Anam Cara.* They worked together, not only in the Big Apple but in such locations as Santa Fe, Boulder, and Seattle. Nóirín said John's entire presence had been nonthreatening. He created a sense of sacred space around any performance. "What I felt about John was that, whatever he said, it was coming from another consciousness," she told me. "When you were with him, it had that feeling of standing on a sacred space or a sacred site. He looked at you. He was visionary and a prophet. He seemed to know what you needed to hear at a particular time. It was almost as though he were embodying a guardian angel. I remember being with him in San Francisco. He was hugely sensitive to the visual art. I would see him in front of a painting with his hands out, just as he would be four hours later in front of an audience, waiting for that inspiration, being open to that experience.

"His was a noninstitutionalized spirituality very much in dialogue and harmony with the cosmos, creation ecology, cosmology. He was a macrocosmological anthem. His theology was holistic, connected with feelings and rituals. He had a huge sense of the feminine within himself and of the role of women in the church." Nóirín Ní Riain said she felt O'Donohue had been gifted with "a touch of the divine" that was always there in his person and being. It reminded her of a meditation by Anthony de Mello entitled "The Empty Chair." In the story, a priest, visiting a patient at home, notices an empty chair by the bedside. The patient says he has placed Jesus on the chair and has been talking to him. He had found prayer difficult until a friend had told him that prayer was a matter of talking to Jesus. He is advised to place an empty chair close to him, to imagine Jesus sitting there, and to converse with him. The patient says he has not had trouble praying since. Some days later, the patient's daughter turns up at the rectory to inform the priest that her father has died. She explains how she had left him alone for a couple of hours but when she returned, she found him dead. But his head had not been resting on the bed but on a chair beside.[7] "Without making him into a saint," explained Nóirín, "when you were with John, there was a presence there, a sense of the divine, and the creating of a sacred space."

A Forgotten Brightness

In his writings, O'Donohue recognizes that the human soul is hungry for beauty, seeking it through landscape or the arts, companionship or religion. When we encounter the Beautiful, there is a sense of homecoming. We feel most alive in its presence because it meets the needs of the soul. In the experience of beauty, we awaken and surrender in the same act and become aware of new ways of being in the world. The wonder of the Beautiful is its ability to surprise. The Greek for "the beautiful" is *to kalon,* related to the word *kalein,* which includes the notion of "call." O'Donohue says that when we experience beauty, we feel called to an awakening of a forgotten brightness. The beauty of the earth is a constant play of light and dark, the visible and the invisible, yet beauty is always more than the senses can perceive. Beauty awakens the soul, and its entrance is the imagination:

> When we bring in the notion of the imagination, we begin to discover a whole new sense of God. The emphasis on guilt, judgment and fear begins to recede. The image of God as a tabloid moral accountant peering into the regions of one's intimate life falls away. The notion of the Divine Imagination brings out the creativity of God, and creativity is the supreme passion of God.[8]

This insight always needs to be balanced against the unknown in God, which remains "beyond the furthest dream of the mind's light." The creation of the world is not God's desire for experimentation. On the contrary, like an artist, God follows his imagination and reaches toward expression:

> Everything that is — every tree, bird, star, stone and wave — existed first as a dream in the mind of the divine artist. Indeed, the world is the mirror of the divine imagination and to decipher the depths of the world is to gain deep insights into the

heart of God. The traces of the divine imagination are everywhere. The beauty of God becomes evident in the beauty of
the world.[9]

O'Donohue told me that he felt religion had become unpopu-
lar because, in its obsession with morality, rules, and regulations, it
had forgotten "the beauty of the mystical flame which is at the
heart of it." In ecological terms, he saw how so much modern
development had desecrated the earth, turning it into a wasteland
because there had been a failure to recognize the sheer beauty of
nature. Beauty had become confused with glamour. Glamour was a
multibillion dollar industry that thrived on dislocating or unhous-
ing people from their own bodies and transferring all the longing
toward the perfection of image. Glamour was insatiable because it
lacked interiority. Beauty was a more sophisticated and substantial
presence with an eternal heart — a threshold place where the ideal
and the real touched each other. People on the bleakest frontiers of
desolation, deprivation, and poverty were often sustained by small
glimpses of beauty.

One of the deepest longings of the human heart, he said, was for
real presence, the goal of truth, the ideal of love, and intentional-
ity of prayer here and in the beatific vision hereafter. Real presence
was the heart of the incarnation and the Eucharist. This was where
imagination worked so beautifully with the absences and empti-
nesses of life, always trying to find a shape of words, music, color,
or stone that would in some way incarnate new presence to fill the
absence. When we experienced real presence, we broke through to
that which was latent and eternal within us but which the daily
round of life kept us away from.

It saddened O'Donohue that, in discussing the Eucharist, the
Catholic hierarchy seemed always to talk about barring certain
groups of people from receiving Holy Communion but never spoke
about the beauty of the sacraments themselves. The cross and the
crucifixion formed a bleak place where no certainty could ever

settle, and its subversive realism was truthful to the depth and power of absence that suffering, pain, and oppression bring to the world. That was the essence of the Eucharist. "In the Eucharist, you have the most amazing symphony of complete presence based on the ultimate absence and the ultimate kind of emptiness," he said. "Sometimes absence creates new possibility. When the carpenter rose from the dead they wanted him to stay around. He said he must go in order to let the spirit come. So, sometimes, that which is absent allows something new to emerge."

Echoing Merton, O'Donohue critiqued modern society as a place where people appeared to inhabit the world of absence, rather than presence, because of technology and virtual reality. Its driven nature turned women and men into the ultimate harvesters of absence. They emerged as ghosts in their own lifetimes. The postmodern mind, particularly, was homeless, haunted by a sense of absence that it could neither understand nor transfigure. Many of the traditional shelters had collapsed. Religion, at least in its official presentation, seemed increasingly to speak in an idiom that was unable (or perhaps unwilling) to converse with the spiritual hunger of the age. Politics appeared devoid of vision and was becoming more and more synonymous with economics. Consumerist culture worshiped accumulation and power, arrogantly creating "its own hollow and gaudy hierarchies."

The imagination occupies a central place in O'Donohue's spiritual landscape because it mirrors the complexity of people's souls. Society and every system, be it religion, politics, or the media, reduce to a common denominator. Only the imagination has the willingness to witness to that which is "really complex, dark, paradoxical, contradictory, and awkward within us, that which does not fit comfortably on the veneer of the social surface." The imagination has the power to trawl and retrieve this poignant and wounded complexity which has to remain hidden. The imagination is faithful to the full home of the heart and all its rooms.

"A Quiet Crucifixion"

O'Donohue usually woke early, went for a walk, did meditation, had breakfast, then settled down to his daily discipline. "In this gable room here, by the fire, looking out onto the lake, is where I usually write," he explained. "I try and show up at the old desk here at about seven thirty or eight o clock in the morning and then begin to get into it. I write everything longhand first and then I put it into the computer afterwards. I can't think and write into a computer at the same time. I also find that I like the words coming from the hand. I like the uniqueness of one's own writing, the way one shapes words. There's also a certain kind of sense of doing the work, when you have to cross out and you've pages that you throw away. At least you see something concrete. And then, finally, when you get a little shape of words that can to some extent hold its own, it's a great pleasure. You might spend five or six hours at it but, if you can get two to three good hours done in a day, that's an awful lot of time."

The practice of writing he described as "strange" because it had somehow to flow naturally. Forced writing was the worst form because there was no life in it. To make a good sentence was "a quiet crucifixion." For him, writing was the purest form of conversation with oneself but, as an act of integrity, it required "incredible watchfulness and discipline to try and write honestly." A book was always conceived in solitude but, once completed, had to find its way to the people who actually needed it. Books were companions to guide people in their lives. They had helped him through "many lonesome and confusing territories." What happened between readers and a particular book was their business.

A book written in the house we were sitting in would echo in many different places, but ultimately it would end up as a private conversation with the reader. The intention was to evoke something that, almost like a poem, was hospitable enough to allow each reader to engage his or her own experience.

Anam Ċara and his subsequent book about belonging, *Eternal Echoes,* are couched in a lyrical-speculative style, where philosophy is wed to poetic evocation. Their purpose is to help people enter the old locked rooms in their own hearts. "How they enter and what they find there is the privilege of their own journey," said O'Donohue. "I believe that life is a huge sacramentality and that the greatest sin is the unlived life. I suppose the more of ourselves that we awaken and the more landscapes within us that we become conscious of, the more we become ourselves and the more we incarnate the destiny that we are meant to walk here. In a certain sense the books are not ideology. There's no program. There's no message. They are just evocations which, hopefully, are very carefully hewn shapes of language to enable people to open doors into their own world."

O'Donohue was not naïve to the fact that readers often expected him to provide solutions to their existential predicaments. Again, he stressed that they should not go on postponing their lives until they were almost finished. It was a matter of discovering the inner path. Even in a crowded train, they could find their inner, private space. He encouraged people to seek the silence within and concentrate, to drink from an inner well that each person had but others could not reach. He encouraged those who might not see a blade of grass or a patch of sky for weeks to retire to the space within, perhaps twice a day. Constantly surprised by the power of thought, he had been into prisons and been moved to tears as he listened to men describing their psychological survival of years in a cell.

Influenced by the fourteenth-century German mystic Meister Eckhart, O'Donohue, then, gently encouraged his readers to look within themselves, rather than set out on a deliberate excursion. There was nothing as near as the eternal:

If there were a spiritual journey, it would be only a quarter-inch long, though many miles deep. It would be a swerve into rhythm with your deeper nature and presence. The wisdom here is so consoling. You do not have to go away outside your self to come into real conversation with your soul and with the mysteries of the spiritual world. The eternal is at home — within you.[10]

It is not surprising then that the author resisted suggestions that he was creating a new spirituality or reclaiming the Celtic tradition for a postmodern audience. He even doubted there was any such thing as spirituality per se. When I asked him about his own spiritual life, he said he was not certain that he actually had one. "I don't know if there is such a thing as a spiritual life. I think all of one's life is eminently spiritual. I think that very often when we talk about a spiritual life we enter into a dualistic kind of thing where we have our normal life and our spiritual life. I think the whole thing is latently creative and eternal. I suppose the faculty that I would consider more spiritual is the imagination because I think it is the actual lyrical and sensuous presence of the soul. I think it's all about the old eternity thing, you know."

What he had tried to initiate in his writings was "a kind of a conversation" that people might or might not pursue. He said he made no claims for his books, except that they could become "mirrors for different individuals on their different ways to get some kind of a glimpse of what is going on within them." The world of the heart and world of the mind were invisible and largely unknown. O'Donohue, then, was an incarnational writer with a sensuous gift for description, image, symbol, and narrative. His work had the soul of speculative reflection and hard-edged conceptual penetration.

Brenda Kimber acquired all O'Donohue's titles as editorial director of Bantam Press in London. She was immediately struck by the originality of the material and the quality of O'Donohue's writing. After signing him, she realized the challenge for both writer and editor would be making the text accessible to readers without oversimplifying the message or compromising the style. "I believe this helped establish him as a major figure in this field," said Brenda Kimber. "John had a very strong and eager audience who were able to connect with him on a number of levels. His handling of the subject of death was extremely positive and helped those who were suffering loss or bereavement. He tried to reach out to people and, in some sense, he may have felt traditional 'religion' was a barrier. So many people today seem disillusioned with traditional forms of religion and turn instead to the commercial world for their comfort. The message transcends physical barriers of countries like America and the United Kingdom. He was concerned about so many issues — commercialism, our treatment of this planet, our lack of respect for the earth and each other as well as the loss of true friendship and family relationships that today seem so broken in comparison to those of the past. I believe John's greatest legacy was his ability to communicate with audiences on a number of important issues. He was a brave, outspoken man — a man with a fine intellect and a generous spirit. He brought love and light to many people."

The Critics and the Clay

But despite the substantial sales of his books, O'Donohue did not work the magic for everyone, and in his lifetime he faced accusations that he was romanticizing the Celtic world. Some said he was a dilettante, dabbling in forms of spiritual aromatherapy. One critic gently mocked his work as a "Valentine's Card" to the nation. "Oh God, I think that's really funny," he roared, when I raised it with him. "I think that, if one can get a sense of scented perfume on the skin from the words that I have written, then there is something else going on that I am not aware of at all." Both *Anam Cara* and *Eternal Echoes* were books with a hard, speculative edge of dense thinking which were tightened and packed into lyrical form. Some might be open to that, he said, while others might not. But if people classified his work in terms of "spiritual aromatherapy," it would seem to his mind that the text did not exist at all. The author also responded to claims that his fusing of European philosophical thought with the Celtic spiritual tradition was contrived. The way Irish sensibility worked, he said, was precisely through the imaginative mold. He wanted to reawaken, reinforce, complement, and counterpoint some of the insights from the Celts with those from the European tradition "and let the two of them come into a conversation with one another." This, he felt, was totally permissible as a form.

During the writing of *Anam Cara,* he had been most afraid of the reaction on home soil because of his respect for "the literate and literary sensibility" of Irish people. He had been, in the end, relieved and moved that people from so many contrasting worlds, from farmers to university professors, had given their warm approval. There were, however, those who derided him for clambering aboard "the Celtic bandwagon" at a time when Ireland was experiencing a period of rapid economic growth known as "the Celtic Tiger." He was not slow to acknowledge the irony: "A bandwagon would be the last thing I could live on in terms of my own personal, intellectual, and emotional integrity," he told me. "I always find myself on different kinds of margins. In a way I suppose I am a kind of solo operator. I find it hard to be part of systems. I am always out on the old edges of things in my own way. They might not be edges others might consider significant, but everyone has to choose their own way."

To those who felt the writer had betrayed Celtic Christianity and had not always been original, O'Donohue explained that the mode of approach and access to such an ancient tradition had been strewn with interpretative difficulties. What he found exceptionally distasteful in New Age spirituality, for example, was the way in which the movement raided past traditions without hermeneutical critique or any sense of distance between the present hunger and the past need. It omitted many symbolic elements of the traditions that it rifled. There was also, for him, a sense in which the Celtic tradition was actually still alive. There were areas in the sensibility and psyche of a people that were atemporal and did not run according to normal chronology.

He went on: "I think in Ireland there is an incredible clay in our minds which is deep-rooted and has a Celtic rhythm to it. I was very aware of this potential hermeneutical difficulty and potential critique. I made it absolutely clear in the preface to my book that this was not a piecemeal scholarly analysis of the Celtic tradition but was intended to initiate a conversation between aspects of the Celtic tradition and our present hungers using the idea and the lens of friendship to begin that. It was based on the epistemological assumption of mine that the Celtic tradition somehow managed to have a lovely, holistic kind of sensibility which did not deny the darkness or the shadows. The scholarly status of the book is the status of a conversation. I think the conversation model is very honorable because it is the infancy of the Western tradition in the dialogues of Plato. The tonality of *Anam Ċara* was primarily toward the creative and the positive — and intended to be so — but not at the expense of the shadow and the darkness."

Ebb and Flow

Although not prone to depression, O'Donohue was no stranger to the darkness of the soul. The most frightening and despairing time of his life was when he lost his faith for six months. He was thankful when it returned but had never felt as forsaken as when it originally floated away. Faith continued to ebb and flow like a tide. As the years went by, O'Donohue found himself having less and less in common with the Roman Catholic hierarchy. The constraints of the institution exasperated him, and he became helplessly disillusioned. O'Donohue felt the institutional church had a pathological fear of the feminine and was "not trustable in relation to eros at all." He believed many of its hierarchical structures ought to be exposed to "the most stringent and rigorous theological questioning." He did not believe church leaders were in step with the march of culture and, even if they had been, felt they would lack the language to converse with it. As he saw it, there was no dialogue between the resources of Catholic heritage and the pressing questions and needs of the present. Nonetheless, it saddened him when people kept discrediting Catholicism because he still found the religion to be "rich, nuanced, luminous, and healing."

When he was a priest, some of his most tender work happened in confessions when people troubled by supposed sins about sexuality were shown they were not sins at all. "You would see their beautiful eros and elemental landscape damaged by a voice outside that had

got falsely into their heads. I have seen couples who didn't get on
and had silence for years and years. Then the shell broke and they
rediscovered each other as though they were young again." He also
said that people who bore illness for decades "in rooms that no one
goes into in houses" conveyed a mystical creativity of the work they
achieved secretly.

Calvary

On the eve of the millennium, Father John O'Donohue spent the
night alone on a mountain, opening his spirit to the possibility
of leaving public ministry, a step he eventually took in November 2000. He had spent many years wrestling with the issue, yet
his friends remained convinced that he never ceased to be a priest
in the sense of his service to, and his living of, a divine vision. He
believed deeply in God and admired the beauty of Catholicism. Its
mystical tradition could hold its own with the best out of Tibet, he
said, and its intellectual tradition was remarkable. He found dogmas fascinating, artistic, speculative, and creative. The substance of
Catholicism had been worked out in conversations with the best
minds of neoclassical antiquity and the medieval times.

One of the loneliest aspects of giving up public priestly ministry
was no longer celebrating the Eucharist. It was an immense loss to
O'Donohue. If we really knew what was going on during a Mass, he
used to say, it would "just blow our minds." The Eucharist was the
place where time and eternity came together. While his celebration
of the dawn Easter Mass in Corcomroe was the climax of the liturgical calendar, Good Friday was "the most haunted day of the year."
There was a loneliness at the center of it that got to the bone in him.
Christ's journey had been so poignant and tender. Here was a young
man with an incredible imagination without which, he told me, we
would know nothing of the Trinity or of God because Christ was
"the doorway to the divine as well as being divine himself." With the
sound of lambs bleating the fields, O'Donohue went on to explain
how Christ had probed and disturbed something at the heart of

human reality that was "utterly once off and completely unique." On that gravity-laden, bleak day Christ had somehow trampled his way up the mountain of Calvary, carrying the loneliness of humankind. As Yeats, Rilke, and other poets had recognized, when "some huge feeling" walked in a place, an imprint was left forever in the ether of that place and in the ether of the world by that person's presence.

Good Friday was a day of absolute silence when the cry went out into the cosmos and no echo returned to any place. Good Friday and Calvary were both a day and place where no certainty could ever settle. The poet loved, though, the slowness of Easter, the patience of it and the fact that "you are made to wait for it." In Conamara, the arrival of Easter Sunday usually coincided with the strengthening of color and the lightness of nature at the heart of springtime.

O'Donohue seemed always conscious that time was short. He wrote and spoke movingly about death. When a person lies down to die, two things are happening for the first time, he would explain: "They are losing the world and they are losing themselves. One of the big privileges of being a priest was to be at the deathbed of people. I think a deathbed is an amazing place. It is anything other than a deathbed. It is a place of incredible transfiguration. Rather than a litany of prayers, a dying person often wants a raft of words to take him to the other shore. If you are humane, trust yourself, and focus on the person who is dying and try to speak to them and listen to them, everything that needs to happen will happen there. At the moment of death, the real event in dying is the invisible event, and it is the soul that takes over in some way. It choreographs the death then. You will see a person who is incredibly frightened and out of somewhere a calm will come... and you don't see what's going on at all. Another thing is happening there."

The consoling effect of O'Donohue's writings was described to me by a bookseller in Galway who had known of people whose traumatic experience of illness and bereavement had been calmed by *Anam Cara*. The author had the special gift of looking at the mountains, valleys, rivers, and seas and being able to give them a spiritual explanation. He remembered a widow who had suffered deeply after her husband had died. She read *Anam Ċara* and, a couple of years later, found herself walking in County Clare, touching the landscape, and using O'Donohue's words. She felt the presence of her husband beside her and was no longer frightened of being alone.

"Recognition of Souls"

During the last year of his life John and his German partner, Kristine Fleck, had talked of making a life together. It was a time of happiness and planning. John had described their extraordinary encounter as a "recognition of souls," which seemed beyond all understanding. Both experienced an immediate sense of homecoming in the sense that they felt they had found their place of belonging at last. Kristine spent time with John in Ireland and, toward the end of 2007, he traveled to France for a holiday near Avignon with Kristine and her family. There, unexpectedly, on January 4, 2008, three days after his fifty-second birthday, John O'Donohue died in his sleep.

The body was flown back to Ireland, where a traditional Irish wake was held. Hundreds came to pay their respects. The funeral took place at St. Patrick's Church, Fanore, County Clare, where John had been baptized. Likened to a farewell for a Gaelic chieftain, the service was attended by his mother, Josie, brothers PJ and Pat, sister Mary, their families, Kristine and her parents, and many close friends. More than two thousand mourners attended the Month's Mind service at Galway Cathedral a few weeks later. John was buried in the heart of the Burren landscape, close to the wild Atlantic Ocean.

For John O'Donohue, death had always been an unknown companion, a presence that accompanied us through life, even though we might not be aware of its nearness. He used to tell people that it was wrong to think about death making an appearance only at the end of life. Our physical death merely completed a process involving this "secret friend" who had been alongside us since our emergence

from the womb. Death could meet us in and through different guises
in the course of our lives, especially in the form of negativity, vulnerability, or psychological pain that exiled us from our own love
and warmth. It was essential to transfigure negativity by "turning it
to the light of your soul." The continual transfiguration of the faces
of our own death would ensure that, at the end of life, our physical
death would be no stranger. With fear overcome, death would be
a meeting with a lifelong friend from the deepest side of our own
nature.

John O'Donohue knew how terrified people were of letting go.
He said they used control as a mechanism to order and structure
their lives and then became trapped in the protective program they
had woven around themselves. This blocked out many blessings. At
times of pain, and particularly at the time of your death, it might
not be possible to maintain such control:

> The mystical life has always recognized that to come deeper
> into the divine presence within, you need to practice detach-
> ment. When you begin to let go, it is amazing how enriched
> your life becomes. False things, which you have desperately
> held on to, move away very quickly from you. Then what is
> real, what you love deeply, and what really belongs to you,
> comes deeper into you. Now no one can ever take them away
> from you.[11]

John O'Donohue was one of the most eloquent and engaging
spiritual writers of modern times. Many felt he had earned a place
in the Christian mystical tradition, but O'Donohue resisted the asso-
ciation. "I wouldn't call myself mystical at all," he told me that day
at his home in Conamara. "But I love the mystics. I trust the mystics
more than any other writers. I think mystics and poets have drawn
the best kind of outlines of where the landscapes of the spiritual
and the eternal actually are. I think that the mystics speak from
within the experience of the eternal rather than speaking about it
from outside. What they speak of, they have lived."

Eternity was moving into a space of distance and rhythm where distance, loneliness, and separation would no longer oppress and you would see those who had gone before. When you were traveling through the tunnel of darkness, when every contour was closed off to you, there would always be the hope that the light would be found within the dark, that the dark would not touch it, and that the door into the light would open for you eventually. That, for John O'Donohue, was the promise of resurrection.

For Absence

May you know that absence is alive with hidden presence,
that nothing is ever lost or forgotten.
May the absences in your life grow full of eternal echo.
May you sense around you the secret Elsewhere
where the presences that have left you dwell.
May you be generous in your embrace of loss.
May the sore well of grief turn into a seamless flow of presence.
May your compassion reach out to the ones we never hear from.
May you have the courage to speak for the excluded ones.
May you become the gracious and passionate subject of your own life.
May you not disrespect your mystery through brittle words or false belonging.
May you be embraced by God in whom dawn and twilight are one.
May your longing inhabit its dreams within the Great Belonging.[12]

Postlude

The master lighting cameraman Freddie Young, who won Academy Awards for his work on *Lawrence of Arabia, Dr. Zhivago,* and *Ryan's Daughter,* was once asked about his working partnership with the film director David Lean. "He gives you an inspiration," said Young, "so you go out of your depth and try and do something extraordinary."[1]

Thomas Merton, Henri J. M. Nouwen, Anthony de Mello, and John O'Donohue were spiritual guides who wrote and spoke out of their own depth, achieving something extraordinary in the process. Cinematographers can create an artificial sense of beauty through painstaking technical expertise and make the ordinary seem extraordinary. Spiritual masters do not make the ordinary extraordinary. They see the extraordinary in the ordinary with such spontaneity that others come naturally to recognize divine beauty in the midst of their everyday lives. Touching people's humanity, they often awaken them to a dormant inner world.

Recognizing the spiritual hunger of the age and detecting the crisis in belonging, these four authors understood the need to connect with people. Sometimes congregations complain that preaching in their churches leaves them cold and bored, especially when the robed figure in the pulpit has become too institutionalized or cerebral. What comes across is a talking collar rather than a speaking person. Then, every so often, they hear a homily (usually at a wedding or funeral) that touches and connects. The church of God immediately springs into life again and they feel close to the divine. Merton, Nouwen, de Mello, and O'Donohue became best-selling writers precisely because they knew *how* to communicate and *who* they were communicating with (not *to*). As Annice Callahan has suggested, spiritual guides invite people to get in touch with their own hearts so they can enable others to get in touch with theirs. They are "symbols of the living God, revering their own mystery and revealing the mystery of God's love through their lives and writings."[2]

Nurtured by the Roman Catholic Church, these four writers respected its foundations and the beauty of its sacramental life, but did not allow themselves to be stultified or constrained by its institutional tentacles. O'Donohue spoke for all four when he defined a priest as being "an artist of the eternal." He believed seminaries produced too many clerics, men who assumed and adopted the uniform, behavior, and language of the institution as they attempted to be priests from the outside in, rather than from the inside out. The cleric was someone insulated against the longings and possibilities of his own humanity. His role subsumed the complexity, conflict, and depth of individual interiority. In contrast to the cleric, the priest was drawn to the frontiers where quest met question, possibility opened to fact, presence transfigured loss, and divinity suffused humanity. Real priesthood at the edge — an identity rather than a role — engaged in a poetics of growth, activating imagination as the primary spiritual faculty to awaken the eternal. A priesthood alive to the imagination found itself in rhythm with the sacrament of life. How true this was of all four and how the underlying import of their writings resonated with a global audience in need of spiritual replenishment, not necessarily mediated through traditional church structures.

As an antidote to the blues of any age, the writings of these men emerged from their own cultural frameworks — and their own struggles — but conveyed an intrinsic message of love and hope unconditioned by time or context. They understood the human condition and opened up pathways to the transcendent. Seeking neither to convert nor indoctrinate, they spoke candidly about God and their own search for truth.

The Archbishop of Canterbury, Dr. Rowan Williams, suggested that the importance of the "Four Evangelists" lay in the fact that they came at questions of meaning in a way that "is not defined by the institution or by the orthodoxy, though they all, in varying degrees, inhabit that world of the church's sacraments, the church's practice, and the church's teaching." They were not theoretical revolutionaries in that sense, but they did not come across as ecclesiastical people. They pushed the boundaries. "All of them in different ways have an extraordinary degree of hospitality to experiences outside their own comfort zone," he said.

The archbishop cited Merton as someone who had been constantly discovering new worlds. Part of the fascination and part of the exasperation with Merton was that, as soon as he had read a book or an article, he had immediately wanted to write about it — "to be there and to be like that." It could be disarming and sometimes a little maddening. Nouwen, of course, shared that characteristic to some extent, although his writings tended to emerge from personal experience. But as Dr. Williams noted: "All of them are very, very rooted people. They all know the language. They know the moves and, in spite of Merton's great rebelliousness about the inherited forms of monasticism, nonetheless he knows it's his home, he knows he's got a base to work from."

In his 2009 Easter sermon, delivered at Canterbury Cathedral a few weeks after our interview, Dr. Williams said that the financial crisis had dealt a heavy blow to the idea that human fulfillment could be thought about merely in terms of material growth and possession. These four writers speak to a time of recession, directing us toward interior transformation and a deeper life in God. In many ways they echo the spirituality of Barack Obama, who sees religion as "transforming, lifelong, and real." Obama embraced the cloak of religion before he took on the mantle of politics. He has said that it was his faith that gave him the will to serve in public office, and it was the worldview of that faith that shaped his understanding of what he would do when he came to power.[3] As Stephen Mansfield pointed out before the new president was elected, Obama was willing to join people of different faiths to solve the crises of his times and tend the wounds of his nation. It was an opportunity to respond to historic wounds and generational conflicts "in the spirit of the great healers."[4] It might, ultimately, "help wed faith to a political vision that leads to meaningful change in our time."[5]

But, as our four "great healers" were all too aware, external change cannot be guaranteed in the long term unless people are prepared to look beyond their own egos and change themselves, to make a difference from the inside out, and to see themselves as part of the whole. And, as President Obama, put it: "At some level, your individual salvation depends on collective salvation. It's only when you hitch yourself up to something bigger than yourself that you're going to realize your true potential, and the world will benefit from that potential."[6]

All four knew only too well that, in any journey toward wholeness, people had to "hitch themselves up" to something larger than themselves. As these profiles have shown, a spirit of gratitude permeated the theology of these writers. Life was a mystery and should not be taken for granted. In his valedictory message to friends, Nouwen said: "Tell everyone I am grateful. I am so very grateful." Gratefulness lies at the mystical core of all religions, providing a point of agreement between people of different traditions that transcends formal dogmas. Every year the Network for Grateful Living, cofounded by the Benedictine monk Brother David Steindl-Rast, has 6.5 million visits to its website (*www.gratefulness.org*) from people in more than 240 countries. It provides education and support for the practice of grateful living as a global ethic. To live gratefully means reaching beyond a sense of entitlement to an appreciation of the gifts people receive moment by moment and a desire to share them with others. It involves a commitment to nonviolence and an awareness of the opportunities available to serve a world in need. The ethic also recognizes a reverence for nature, and for other people and their customs.

The universal sentiment of gratefulness is shared by all cultures and religious traditions. Like the spiritual writings of Merton, Nouwen, de Mello, and O'Donohue, it provides a common language for dialogue between religious people and nonreligious people. The ethic teaches people to appreciate what they have, especially in a time of recession, and has become a springboard for relieving "the fear of scarcity that drives all unsustainable consumption patterns." Although the organization is non-profit-making and without political affiliation, it sees in Barack Obama's presidency "a great advance in intercultural respect, world citizenship, and our shared call to service." The same might be said of the four authors. "We need to recognize that development of a creative inner life is a lifelong pursuit that takes as many forms as there are people," said executive director Patricia Carlson. "The practice of grateful living — a moment-by-moment awareness of life's gifts — is the exact difference between seeing the glass as half full rather than half empty, as the metaphor goes. The impact of this attitude on the collective consciousness of a nation cannot be overestimated."

Jazz, they say, is about "peeling away the layers of artifice to get at what is," an opportunity to explore the sense of soul "at its most profound center."[7] In its own distinctive forms, the spiritual writing of all four authors explored the heart of divine–human encounter, releasing and empowering readers to grow closer to God — and their true selves — in the process. For Thomas Merton, Henri Nouwen, Anthony de Mello, and John O'Donohue, this authentic search for interior truth and freedom became the hallmark, endearing them to their audience as spiritual masters for all seasons.

Who are the prophets?
They are a royal people,
who penetrate mystery
and see with the spirit's eyes.

In illuminating darkness they speak out.

They are living, penetrating clarity.
They are a blossom blooming only
on the shoot that is rooted
in the flood of light.

—Hildegard of Bingen

OTHER BOOKS BY MICHAEL FORD

*Father Mychal Judge**

*Song of the Nightingale**

Wounded Prophet

Disclosures

Eternal Seasons (editor)

The Dance of Life (editor)

A Restless Soul (editor)

---

*Published by Paulist Press.

Notes

Prelude

1. John O'Donohue, *Benedictus: A Book of Blessings* (London: Bantam Press, 2007), 161–62.
2. Michael Ford, *Wounded Prophet: A Portrait of Henri J. M. Nouwen* (New York: Doubleday, 1999).

1 / Unmasking the Self: The Faces of Thomas Merton

1. Thomas Merton, *First and Last Thoughts: A Thomas Merton Reader*, ed. Thomas P. McDonnell (New York: Image, 1989), 16.
2. Father Kenneth Leech, conference on Thomas Merton, London, May 2, 1987.
3. Thomas Merton, *New Seeds of Contemplation* (New York: New Directions, 2007), 25.
4. Ibid., 5.
5. Ibid., 52.
6. Thomas Merton, *The Intimate Merton: His Life from His Journals*, ed. Patrick Hart and Jonathan Montaldo (San Francisco: HarperSanFrancisco, 2002), 266.
7. Thomas Merton, *Conjectures of a Guilty Bystander* (London: Burns & Oates, 1968), 84.
8. Ibid., 211.
9. Ibid., 275.
10. Thomas Merton, "The Root of War," *Catholic Worker*, October 28, 1961, as quoted in *The Pocket Thomas Merton*, ed. Robert Inchausti (Boston: New Seeds Books, 2005), 176–77.
11. Republished in a collection of essays, *Seeds of Destruction* (New York: Farrar, Straus and Giroux, 1980), 228.
12. Ibid., 228–29.
13. Ibid., 231.
14. Merton, *New Seeds of Contemplation*, 1.
15. *A Thomas Merton Reader*, ed. McDonnell, Thomas P. (New York: Harcourt, Brace & World, 1962), 302–3.
16. *The Asian Journal of Thomas Merton* (New York: New Directions, 1973), 233–35.

17. Joan C. McDonald, *Tom Merton: A Personal Biography* (Milwaukee: Marquette University Press, 2006).
18. Ibid., 252.
19. Thomas Merton, *A Life in Letters*, ed. William H. Shannon and Christine M. Bochen (New York: HarperCollins, 2008), 327.
20. Thomas Merton, *The Hidden Ground of Love: The Letters of Thomas Merton on Religious Experience and Social Concerns*, selected and ed. William H. Shannon (New York: Harcourt, 1993), 156–58, as quoted in William H. Shannon, *Thomas Merton: An Introduction* (Cincinnati: St. Anthony Messenger Press, 2005), 170–71.

2 / The Monk and the Archbishop: A Conversation about Merton with Dr. Rowan Williams

1. René Girard was professor of French language, literature, and civilization at Stanford University from 1981 to 1995. His book *Violence and the Sacred* explored the nature of human evil.
2. Thomas Merton, *The Road to Joy: Letters to New and Old Friends* (New York: Farrar, Straus, Giroux, 1980), 239.
3. Thomas Merton, *Conjectures of a Guilty Bystander* (London: Burns & Oates, 1968), 308–9.
4. Thomas Merton, *The Sign of Jonas* (London: Hollis & Carter, 1953), 177.
5. Thomas Merton, "Marxism and Monastic Perspectives," from *The Asian Journal of Thomas Merton* (New York: New Directions, 1975), 343.
6. William Apel, *Signs of Peace: The Interfaith Letters of Thomas Merton* (Maryknoll, NY: Orbis Books, 2006), 9.

3 / Trusting the Heart: The Dynamics of Henri J. M. Nouwen

1. Henri J. M. Nouwen, *Reaching Out: The Three Movements of the Spiritual Life* (London: Fount, 1980), 16.
2. Henri Nouwen, *Turn My Mourning into Dancing: Finding Hope in Hard Times*, ed. Timothy Jones (Nashville: World Publishing, 2001), 25–26.
3. Henri J. M. Nouwen, *Our Greatest Gift: A Meditation on Dying and Caring* (New York: HarperCollins 1994), 67.
4. Henri J. M. Nouwen, *The Way of the Heart* (London: Darton, Longman and Todd, 1990), 76.
5. Ibid., 77.

6. "Life Is Now: A Conversation with Henri J. M. Nouwen," *Fellowship* (December 1984): 6.

7. Henri J. M. Nouwen, "The Trusting Heart and the Primacy of the Mystical Life," *New Oxford Review* 53 (October 1986): 6.

8. Michael Ford, *Wounded Prophet: A Portrait of Henri J. M. Nouwen* (New York: Doubleday, 1999).

9. Henri J. M. Nouwen, *The Inner Voice of Love: A Journey through Anguish to Freedom* (New York: Doubleday, 1996), xvi–xviii.

10. Ibid., 97.

11. Henri J. M. Nouwen, "Control Your Own Drawbridge," from *The Inner Voice of Love,* 84–85.

12. Henri J. M. Nouwen, *Can You Drink the Cup?* (Notre Dame, IN: Ave Maria Press, 1996), 33–34.

13. Henri J. M. Nouwen, *In the Name of Jesus: Reflections on Christian Leadership* (London: Darton, Longman and Todd, 1989), 43–44.

4 / The Monk and the Professor: Conversations about Merton and Nouwen

1. Thomas Merton, *Learning to Love: The Journals of Thomas Merton,* vol. 6, *Exploring Solitude and Freedom,,* ed. Christine M. Bochen (San Francisco: HarperSanFrancisco, 1998), 232.

2. Henri J. M. Nouwen, *Thomas Merton: Contemplative Critic* (New York: Triumph Books, 1991), 3.

3. Henri J. M. Nouwen, *The Genesee Diary: Report from a Trappist Monastery* (New York: Image, 1981).

4. Ibid., 183–84.

5. Jim Forest, *Living with Wisdom: A Life of Thomas Merton,* rev. ed. (Maryknoll, NY: Orbis Books, 2008).

6. Henri J. M. Nouwen, *Behold the Beauty of the Lord: Praying with Icons* (Notre Dame, IN: Ave Maria Press, 1987).

5 / Deconditioning the Mind: The Awakening of Anthony de Mello

1. Anthony de Mello, *The Song of the Bird* (New York: Image, 1984), 3–4.

2. Anthony de Mello, "Being a Changed Person," Anthony de Mello website: *www.demello.org.*

3. Aurel Brys, SJ, and Joseph Pulickal, SJ, eds. *We Heard the Bird Sing: Interacting with Anthony de Mello* (Chicago: Loyola University Press, 1995), 14.

4. Anthony de Mello, "We All Depend upon Each Other," Anthony de Mello website: *www.demello.org.*

5. Anthony de Mello, "Seeing People as They Are — Not as I Wish Them to Be," Anthony de Mello website: *www.demello.org.*

6. Brys and Pulickal, *We Heard the Bird Sing*, 85.

7. de Mello, *Song of the Bird*, 102.

8. Anthony de Mello, *Sadhana: A Way to God* (New York: Image, 1984), 41.

9. Anthony de Mello, *The Prayer of the Frog*, vol. 1 (Anand, India: Gujarat Sahitya Prakash, 1993), xxi.

10. de Mello, *Sadhana*, 8.

11. de Mello, *Prayer of the Frog*, 45.

12. de Mello, *Song of the Bird*, unnumbered.

13. Ibid., 39.

14. Anand Nayak, *Anthony de Mello: His Life and His Spirituality* (Dublin: Columba Press, 2007), 47

15. Brys and Pulickal, *We Heard the Bird Sing*, 103.

16. Carlos G. Vallés, SJ, *Unencumbered by Baggage: Father Anthony de Mello, a Prophet for Our Times* (Anand, India: Gujarat Sahitya Prakash, 1987).

17. Carlos Vallés, *Diez Años Después: Reflexiones sobre Anthony de Mello* (Madrid: San Pablo, 1998).

18. Nayak, *Anthony de Mello*.

19. Cardinal Joseph Ratzinger, prefect, and Archbishop Tarcisio Bertone, secretary, *Notification Concerning the Writings of Father Anthony de Mello SJ* (Rome: Congregation for the Doctrine of the Faith, June 24, 1998), 1.

20. Ibid., 2.

21. Nayak, *Anthony de Mello*, 8.

22. Ibid., 209–11 passim.

23. Ursula King, *The Search for Spirituality: Our Global Quest for a Spiritual Life* (New York: BlueBridge, 2008), 62–63.

24. Anthony de Mello spirituality conference, as quoted by William Dych, SJ, in *Anthony de Mello: Writings*, Modern Spiritual Masters Series (Maryknoll, NY: Orbis Books, 1999), 107.

25. de Mello, *Song of the Bird*, 1.

6 / Befriending the Soul: The Landscapes of John O'Donohue

1. John O'Donohue, "Fluent," in *Conamara Blues* (London: Bantam Books, 2001), 41.

2. From a radio interview, as quoted by John Skinner in his obituary of O'Donohue, *The Independent* (London), February 27, 2008.

3. John O'Donohue, *Anam Ċara* (London: Bantam Press, 1997), 121.

4. John O'Donohue, *Eternal Echoes: Exploring Our Hunger to Belong* (London: Bantam Press, 1998), xvii–xviii.

5. O'Donohue, *Anam Ċara*, 38.

6. A reference to the Irish writer James Stephens.

7. Anthony de Mello, *Sadhana: A Way to God; Christian Exercises in Eastern Form* (New York: Image 1984), 78.

8. John O'Donohue, *Divine Beauty: The Invisible Embrace* (London: Bantam Press, 2003), 140.

9. Ibid., 141.

10. O'Donohue, *Anam Ċara*, 120.

11. Ibid., 246.

12. John O'Donohue, "A Blessing for Absence," in *Benedictus: A Book of Blessings* (London: Bantam Press, 2007), 62.

Postlude

1. Freddie Young, as quoted on the Internet Encyclopaedia of Cinematographers.

2. Annice Callahan, RSCJ, *Spiritual Guides for Today* (London: Darton, Longman and Todd, 1992), 17.

3. Stephen Mansfield, *The Faith of Barack Obama* (Nashville: Thomas Nelson, 2008), 143.

4. Ibid., 132.

5. Ibid., 144.

6. Barack Obama, August 10, 2006, as quoted in *Barack Obama: In His Own Words*, ed. Lisa Rogak (London: JR Books, 2009), 123.

7. Geoffrey C. Ward and Ken Burns, *Jazz: A History of America's Music* (New York: Alfred A. Knopf, 2000), ix.

Selected Bibliography

Apel, William. *Signs of Peace: The Interfaith Letters of Thomas Merton.* Maryknoll, NY: Orbis Books, 2006.

Atkinson, Morgan C., with Jonathan Montaldo. *Soul Searching: The Journey of Thomas Merton.* Collegeville, MN: Liturgical Press, 2008.

Bamberger, John Eudes, OCSO. *Thomas Merton: Prophet of Renewal.* Kalamazoo, MI: Cistercian Publications, 2005.

Bianchi, Enzo. *Words of Spirituality: Towards a Lexicon of the Inner Life.* London: SPCK, 2002.

Callahan, Annice, RSCJ. *Spiritual Guides for Today.* London: Darton, Longman and Todd, 1992.

———. *Spiritualities of the Heart.* Mahwah, NJ: Paulist Press, 1990.

Cunningham, Lawrence S. *Thomas Merton and the Monastic Vision.* Grand Rapids: Wm B. Eerdmans, 1999.

de Mello, Anthony. *Anthony de Mello: Writings.* Ed. William Dych, SJ. Maryknoll, NY: Orbis Books, 1999.

———. *The Prayer of the Frog.* Vol. 1. Anand, India: Gujarat Sahitya Prakash, 1993.

———. *Sadhana: A Way to God; Christian Exercises in Eastern Form.* New York: Image, 1984.

———. *The Song of the Bird.* New York: Image, 1984.

———. *Wellsprings: A Book of Spiritual Exercises.* New York: Image, 1986.

De Wilde, Laurent. *Monk.* New York: Marlowe & Company, 1997.

Downey, Michael, ed. *The New Dictionary of Catholic Spirituality.* Collegeville, MN: Liturgical Press, 1993.

Durback, Robert, ed. *Seeds of Hope: A Henri Nouwen Reader.* New edition. London: Darton, Longman and Todd, 1998.

Ford, Michael. *Wounded Prophet: A Portrait of Henri J. M. Nouwen.* New York: Doubleday, 1999.

Forest, Jim. *Living with Wisdom: A Life of Thomas Merton.* Rev. ed. Maryknoll, NY: Orbis Books, 2008.

Forsthoefel, Thomas A. *The Dalai Lama: Essential Writings*. Maryknoll, NY: Orbis Books, 2008.

Furlong, Monica. *Thomas Merton: A Biography*. London: Darton, Longman and Todd, 1985.

Georgiou, S. T. *Mystic Street: Meditations on a Spiritual Path*. Ottawa: Novalis, 2007.

———. *The Way of the Dreamcatcher: Spirit Lessons with Robert Lax: Poet, Peacemaker, Sage*. Ottawa: Novalis, 2002.

Greer, Wendy Wilson, ed. *Henri J. M. Nouwen, The Only Necessary Thing: Living a Prayerful Life*. New York: Crossroad, 1999, London: Darton, Longman and Todd, 2000.

Hart, Patrick, and Jonathan Montaldo. *The Intimate Merton: His Life from His Journals*. Oxford: Lion Publishing, 2002.

Inchausti, Robert, ed. *Echoing Silence: Thomas Merton and the Vocation of Writing*. Boston: New Seeds, 2007.

———, ed.*The Pocket Thomas Merton*. Boston: New Seeds, 2005.

King, Ursula. *The Search for Spirituality: Our Global Quest for a Spiritual Life*. New York: BlueBridge, 2008.

Leech, Kenneth. *True God: An Exploration in Spiritual Theology*. London: Sheldon Press, 1985.

Mansfield, Stephen. *The Faith of Barack Obama*. Nashville: Thomas Nelson, 2008.

Martin, James, SJ. *Becoming Who You Are: Insights on the True Self from Thomas Merton and Other Saints*. Mahwah, NJ: HiddenSpring, 2006.

McDonald, Joan C. *Tom Merton: A Personal Biography*. Milwaukee: Marquette University Press, 2006.

McDonnell, Thomas P., ed. *A Thomas Merton Reader*. Rev. ed. New York: Image Books, 1996.

Merton, Thomas. *The Asian Journal of Thomas Merton*. New York: New Directions, 1973.

———. *Conjectures of a Guilty Bystander*. London: Burns & Oates, 1968.

———. *New Seeds of Contemplation*. New York: New Directions, 2007.

———. *The Seven Storey Mountain*. New York: Harcourt, Brace and Company, 1948.

———. *The Sign of Jonas*. London: Hollis & Carter, 1953.

————. *Thomas Merton: A Life in Letters, The Essential Collection.* Ed. William H. Shannon and Christine M. Bochen. New York: HarperCollins, 2008.

————. *Thoughts in Solitude.* London: Burns & Oates, 1984.

Mott, Michael. *The Seven Mountains of Thomas Merton.* Boston: Houghton Mifflin, 1984.

Nayak, Anand. *Anthony de Mello: His Life and Spirituality.* Dublin: Columba Press, 2007.

Nouwen, Henri J. M. *Behold the Beauty of the Lord: Praying with Icons.* Notre Dame, IN: Ave Maria Press, 1987.

————. *A Cry for Mercy: Prayers from the Genesee.* Maryknoll, NY: Orbis Books, 1981.

————. *The Dance of Life: Weaving Sorrows and Blessings into One Joyful Step.* Ed. Michael Ford. Notre Dame, IN: Ave Maria Press, 2005.

————. *Eternal Seasons: A Spiritual Journey through the Church's Year.* Ed. Michael Ford. Notre Dame, IN: Ave Maria Press, 2007.

————. *The Genesee Diary: Report from a Trappist Monastery.* New York: Image Books, 1981.

————. *The Inner Voice of Love: A Journey through Anguish to Freedom.* New York: Doubleday, 1996.

————. *In the Name of Jesus: Reflections on Christian Leadership.* London: Darton, Longman and Todd, 1989.

————. Introduction. *Desert Wisdom: Sayings from the Desert Fathers.* Trans. and art by Yushi Nomura. Maryknoll, NY: Orbis Books, 2001.

————. *Life of the Beloved: Spiritual Living in a Secular World.* London: Hodder & Stoughton, 1993.

————. *Reaching Out: The Three Movements of the Spiritual Life.* London: Fount, 1980.

————. *A Restless Soul: Meditations from the Road.* Ed. Michael Ford. Notre Dame, IN: Ave Maria Press, 2008.

————. *The Return of the Prodigal Son: A Story of Homecoming.* London: Darton, Longman and Todd, 1996.

————. *Thomas Merton: Contemplative Critic.* New York: Triumph Books, 1991.

————. *The Way of the Heart.* London: Darton, Longman and Todd, 1990.

Obama, Barack. *The Audacity of Hope.* New York: Crown Publishers, 2006.

————. *Dreams from My Father.* New York: Crown Publishers, 2004.

————. *In His Own Words.* Ed. Lisa Rogak. New York: Carroll & Graf, 2007.

O'Connell, Patrick F., ed. *The Vision of Thomas Merton.* Notre Dame, IN: Ave Maria Press, 2003.

O'Donohue, John. *Anam Ċara .* London: Bantam Press, 1997.

————. *Benedictus: A Book of Blessings.* London: Bantam Press, 2007.

————. *Divine Beauty: The Invisible Embrace.* London: Bantam Press, 2003.

————. *Eternal Echoes: Exploring Our Hunger to Belong.* London: Bantam Press, 1998.

Pennington, M. Basil, OCSO. *The Cistercians.* Collegeville, MN: Liturgical Press, 1992.

————. *Thomas Merton My Brother: His Journey to Freedom, Compassion, and Final Integration.* London: New City, 1996.

Shannon, William H. *Thomas Merton: An Introduction.* Cincinnati: St. Anthony Messenger Press, 1997, revised ed., 2005.

————, Christine M. Bochen, and Patrick F. O'Connell. *The Thomas Merton Encyclopedia.* Maryknoll, NY: Orbis Books, 2002.

Thien-An, Thich. *Zen Philosophy, Zen Practice.* Berkeley, Calif.: Dharma Publishing, 1975.

Twomey, Gerald, ed. *Thomas Merton: Prophet in the Belly of a Paradox.* New York: Paulist Press, 1978.

Uhl⌐   Santa Fe, NM:

V⌐   ⌐*ny de Mello,*
                                                       tya Prakash,

5823   *a's Music.*